UMAIR MUHAMMAD

Confronting Injustice

Confronting Injustice

*Social Activism in the Age of
Individualism*

UMAIR MUHAMMAD

Haymarket Books
Chicago, IL

First published by Muhammad, Umair

This edition published in 2016 by
Haymarket Books
P.O. Box 180165
Chicago, IL 60618
773-583-7884
www.haymarketbooks.org
info@haymarketbooks.org

ISBN: 978-1-60846-570-5

Book design by Alexandra Fox. Cover design by Rachel Cohen.

Trade distribution:
In the US, Consortium Book Sales and Distribution,
www.cbsd.com
In Canada, Publishers Group Canada, www.pgcbooks.ca
In the UK, Turnaround Publisher Services,
www.turnaround-uk.com
All other countries, Publishers Group Worldwide,
www.pgw.com

This book was published with the generous support of Lannan
Foundation and Wallace Action Fund.

Printed in Canada by union labor.

Library of Congress Cataloging-in-Publication data is available.

10 9 8 7 6 5 4 3 2 1

Waitin' for when the last shall be first and the first shall be last

In a cardboard box 'neath the underpass

—Bruce Springsteen

Contents

Acknowledgements

The love and support of my parents is a crucial element in all of my undertakings, including this book.

I am indebted to Connor Allaby, Cyril Francis, Pascal Genest-Richard, Patricia Hoyeck, Khalil Martin, Daniel Miller, Brayden McNeill, Filzah Nasir, Saqib Naveed, Jennifer Nowoselski, Rahat Rahman, Elmira Reisi, Vinay Sagar, and Gajan Sathananthan for reading all or parts of the original manuscript and offering helpful comments. The early drafts of the book were greatly improved because of their criticisms and advice. My thanks to Jordyn Marcellus for copy-editing and to Alexandra Fox for taking on numerous tasks required to get the original edition of the book published.

Without the encouragement given by John Riddell and Suzanne Weiss, the present edition of the book would likely not have come into existence. Also, without them, the original edition would have gotten a lot less attention.

Everyone I have had a chance to interact with at Haymarket Books is great. I especially need to thank John McDonald, who encouraged me to send in the manuscript, as well as Anthony Arnove and Dao X. Tran, both of whom did not seem to mind too much when I didn't send things in on time or when I overlooked certain tasks. Thanks are also due to Rachel Cohen, Eric Kerl, and many others behind the scenes at Haymarket with whom I have not directly interacted.

Sadia Khan is the reason the afterword makes any sense whatsoever.

This book is dedicated to my mother's late sister, Rukhsana—Chhana Khala, as she was known to me. Her passing served as a painful reminder that I am much too far away from home. I am grateful that I was able to visit and spend time with her a few years ago. Her deep sense of justice will remain an inspiration.

The original edition of the book was made possible by an online crowd-funding campaign to which dozens of people contributed. I would like to thank the following people in particular for their generous contributions:

Majd Al-Shihabi
Connor Allaby
Joe Chellakudam
Kyle Eckart
Chanakya Gupta
Zeeshan Haider
Tanya Herbert
Mahmoud Khattab
Angela Ko
David Lalanne
Kaitlynn Livingstone
Ewelina Luczko
Yiannis Loizides
Evan MacAdam
Patrick Miller

Navninder Mokha
Filzah Nasir
Viraj Ranjankumar
Chelsey Rhodes
George Roter
Vinay Sagar
Gajan Sathananthan
Mohamed Sidahmed
Marc-André Simard
Adam Spilka
Waterloo Public Interest
Research Group
Obaidullah Younas
Aftad Zaman

Introduction

In his 1969 novel *Slaughterhouse-Five*, Kurt Vonnegut tells of an acquaintance who chided him for writing an anti-war book: "Why don't you write an anti-*glacier* book instead?"

"What he meant, of course," Vonnegut writes, "was that there would always be wars, that they were as easy to stop as glaciers."[1]

Vonnegut was wrong. Hardly anyone could have known it at the time but it turns out that glaciers are quite a bit easier to stop than wars. Not only have we become proficient at stopping glaciers, we have forced a great number of them into rapid retreat. All we had to do was release massive amounts of greenhouse gases into the atmosphere by burning fossil fuels at manic rates—par for the course as far as modern civilization seems to be concerned. It would be wonderful if right about now we could also come up with a way to stop wars. Otherwise, humanity will soon find itself in more than a bit of trouble.

Consider, for example, the fate connected to the rapidly melting glaciers in Tibet. These glaciers are the source of a significant number of Asia's major rivers and support the livelihoods of 1.4 billion people.[2] As they continue to melt and the water supplies in the rivers they feed become progressively unreliable, the threat of conflict over the already-contested transboundary rivers in the region will be greatly heightened. Countries will be increasingly inclined to build dams to manage erratic flows and stop the water from getting downstream. It just so happens that three of the countries that share Tibetan waterways—China, India, and Pakistan—possess nuclear weapons. We can be certain that unless meaningful action is taken in advance by the concerned parties in the region to prevent conflict, countless human beings will lose their lives in possibly-nuclear water wars. So it goes.

Unfortunately for us, dire scenarios like this one are not unique to Asia. They can be found across the planet.[3] But even if we disregard the threat of wars over dwindling resources, the global environmental destruction we are creating threatens to crush us under its weight. According to the United Nations, three billion additional people may be pushed into extreme poverty by 2050 unless the environmental devastation connected with global warming can be averted.[4] If allowed to persist, before long climate change could very well mean the end of our species.

Humanity faces a crisis on a scale unlike any it has encountered in the past. Those who are alive today have the power to ensure that human beings have a desirable future on this planet. We can accomplish this historic task or we can condemn succeeding generations to utter misery and, ultimately, to nonexistence.

Of course, to present existing humanity as a homogenous collective by referring to it as "those who are alive today" is the wrong way to approach the environmental crisis. In no way are all of us equally responsible for having created the problem. What is more, the burdens of a ruined environment, at least in the short term, will not be borne equally. A minority of human beings—the rich—have been largely responsible for creating climate change. And those who have contributed least to the problem stand to suffer the most as a result of it. The poor, as usual, will disproportionately bear the adverse consequences of actions taken by the wealthy.

Noting that one day seven billion people will live on the planet in *Slaughterhouse-Five*, Vonnegut offers the following reflection: "I suppose they will all want dignity."[5] In 2011, the world's population did cross the seven-billion mark and, as all of these beings are human, we can indeed be sure that they want a dignified existence. Countless numbers of them are currently denied it. Climate change poses a serious threat to a desirable future for the mass of humanity, but for too many people on our planet *the present* happens to be undesirable. If climate change is an acute crisis, global poverty is a chronic one. Hundreds of millions continue to lack access to basic amenities like food, water, sanitation, shelter, and healthcare at a time when indescribable amounts of wealth have been amassed. The past half-century has witnessed repeated pronouncements being made in every corner of the world about the need to reduce poverty. Despite this, and despite the resources we have had at our disposal, progress in the fight against poverty has been painfully slow.

South Asia and sub-Saharan Africa in particular have had a difficult time with poverty-reduction. By contrast in East Asia, most recently especially in China, there has been noteworthy progress. China has relied on its abundance of cheap labor to attain its famed status as "the workshop of the world." Becoming a manufacturing powerhouse has allowed the country to pull millions out of poverty. But all is not good news. At the same time as incredible growth rates have been realized, an environmental catastrophe has been unleashed. Outdoor air pollution led to 1.2 million premature deaths in China in 2010, accounting for about 40 percent of the global total.[6] The country's rivers have been ravaged by industrial waste—in 2012, the head of the ministry of water resources admitted that two-fifths of China's rivers were "seriously polluted."[7] Perhaps most troubling of all, China has of late surpassed the U.S. to become the leading emitter of carbon dioxide in the world.[8]

Chinese government officials justifiably point out that in terms of cumulative per capita emissions their country still lags far behind the West. In the face of the gravity of the climate crisis, however, such statements are little more than pretences to avoid making the needed reductions in greenhouse gas emissions. China's posturing is certainly more defensible than that of Western countries, which have likewise declined to make meaningful reductions. But at the end of the day, unless the largest emitters are willing to make drastic cuts, the world is doomed.

Given that poverty is still rife in China, and that making the necessary cuts in emissions would no doubt get in the way of the country's poverty-reduction strategy, are we forced to conclude that environmental limits make it impossible to meaningfully improve the living standards of the poor? Is it the case that there are just too many people on the planet, making poverty-reduction and global environmental sustainability two mutually exclusive options?

Overpopulation often finds itself being presented as a major obstacle to global sustainability. The focus on population is, however, misplaced. *Overconsumption*, not overpopulation, is the problem. And only the rich are partaking in the consumption frenzy. According to Princeton University's Stephen Pacala, the wealthiest 500 million people are responsible for 50 percent of all greenhouse gas emissions.[9] ("These people are really rich by global standards. Every single one of them earns more than the average American and they also occur in all the countries of the world. There are Chinese and Americans and Europeans and Japanese and Indians all in this group.")

"The poorest 3 billion people ... emit essentially nothing," Pacala points out.[10] Those who are impoverished could appreciably increase their consumption, as well as their emissions, and still not create a significant burden on the global environment. The rich, on the other hand, must radically reduce their consumption levels. Except, of course, the problem is that most poverty-reduction schemes involve putting the poor to work to produce goods for those with wealth. What hope would the poor have of escaping poverty if the rich were to change their lavish ways? To be sure, such a scenario would result in even the relatively well-off suffering greatly.

The fact that these are the prospects we are faced with should start to clue us into the absurdity of our current social arrangement. The health of the environment cannot allow the rich to remain engaged in hyper-consumption. But putting an end to this behavior while remaining within the bounds of the existing arrangement would result in destitution for most of humanity. Why, then, should we remain within the bounds of the existing arrangement? "Any fool," the sociologist and mathematician Johan Galtung writes, "can build an economic system where rich people buy expensive products."[11] It is time for us to stop being foolish and build something better.

THE CRISIS OF ACTIVISM

Precisely at a time when we need it most, bold and imaginative activism has made itself difficult to find. It is not the case that activism in general is in short supply. One finds, in fact, that activist ideals and vocabulary have securely made their way into everyday life. But this has happened in a way that has left society fundamentally unchanged. It is the messages communicated by activists, on the other hand, that have been distorted and have regularly found themselves being used to reinforce the social realities they were originally devised to change.

Perhaps the most blatant example of the co-optation of activist ideals can be seen in the supposed embrace of the concept of sustainability by the corporate world. Oil companies long ago discovered the public relations benefits of describing their operations with the use of phrases such as "sustainable development" and "sustainable growth."[12] More recently we have witnessed the extraordinary rise in the consumption of plastic bottled water, soon after which came bottled water for those who are environmentally conscious. Or so companies like Nestlé, which eagerly promotes the fact that its bottles now contain "25 percent less plastic," would have us believe.[13]

The watering down, emptying out, and distortion of activist ideals has been helped along by activists. For one thing, we have too often been willing to ignore the *social* dimensions of the problems that confront us, believing instead in the idea that the actions of autonomous *individuals* have led us to our current impasse. A corrective is offered for this faulty outlook in the following chapters. I argue that social realities, in particular those created to meet the needs of our economic system, constrain and direct the actions of individuals. It is these social realities, therefore, that must attract most of our attention when we struggle to create change, even when reorienting the behavior of individuals happens to be our ultimate aim.

Living within a social system dominated by the market, it is no coincidence that so many of us have adopted an individualist outlook. The routine of market exchange between individuals who are driven by self-interest has conditioned us to see human society as a collection of disconnected and primarily self-interested individuals. What is troubling is that so many activists have reconciled themselves to this vision of society, and have set about working to reinforce its presence. They have come to champion the values and features of the existing arrangement. In other words, those who have set out to change things are instead working to keep them from changing.

This is especially the case within the professionalized, bureaucratized world of non-governmental organizations (NGOs). Among NGOs, one can easily find not only tacit support for the values of our age, but explicit devotion to them. In place of a commitment to meaningful social change, there exists an insistence on conducting piecemeal charity, an obedient faith in technocratic solutions, as well as an idealization of the marketplace and the corporate realm. "Increasingly the model for the 'successful' NGO," Brian Murphy notes, "is the corporation—ideally a transnational corporation—and NGOs are ever more marketed and judged against corporate ideals."[14]

TOWARD GLOBAL TRANSFORMATION

The change we need will not be arrived at if we stick to the kind of activism that is commonplace today. We need to dissociate ourselves from individualism and embrace the social. We need to move beyond the local and seek the global. We need to see the numerous struggles against injustice around the world as part of a wider struggle for global transformation. But *seeing* them as such does not make them so. We also need to *work* to help the numerous smaller struggles coalesce into a large global struggle.

If readers find statements calling for a "global transformation" to be too idealistic and unreasonable, I hope by the time they have finished this book to have convinced them otherwise. I hope to make clear that the structures of our existing social arrangement disallow it to meet the needs of our time. The most reasonable thing to do is to work towards a goal that is considered unreasonable by prevailing standards.

CHAPTER 1

The Age of Individualism

*Our system is one of detachment: to keep
silenced people from asking questions, to keep
the judged from judging, to keep solitary people
from joining together, and the soul from putting
together its pieces.*

—Eduardo Galeano[1]

Our present age is alternately referred to through the use of various words and phrases: neoliberalism, market fundamentalism, the age of inequality, as well as others. All of these stand fundamentally for the same thing. The Indian journalist Palagummi Sainath explains, "You can call it what you like. Some people call it neoliberalism. Some people call it corporate globalization … Some of us with a more limited vocabulary, we call it capitalism."[2] The different descriptors of our age may refer to a specific aspect, phase, brand, or result of capitalism, but at the end of the day, capitalism is what it is. The same is true for the phrase I have chosen. "The age of individualism" is used here to denote the cultural values that have arisen out of capitalism.

Capitalism is often thought of strictly as an economic system in which production is held under private ownership and control. A more complete evaluation, however, requires us to regard it as an entire social system. It not only determines the ways in which we engage with each other in the economic sphere, but in all aspects of our lives. In its quest to sustain perpetual growth, capitalism commodifies all that it can. It turns interactions and activities that were once outside the reach of the market into things that have dollar signs attached to them, and it continuously brings needs into being where none previously existed.

Prevailing opinion regards the age of individualism as an altogether good thing. The cultural values that have accompanied modern capitalism are celebrated and a triumphant narrative has been devised to explain the virtues of our age. We are told that our culture prizes the individual over and above society. The individual has been set free, in the sense that the market supposedly gives her *equal opportunity* to fulfill her desires—crucially, we are told that no one will get in her way, and she cannot come in the way of anyone else. Our concept of individual freedom is, hence, rooted in the following principle: "You stay out of my way, and I will stay out of yours."[3]

It is plainly evident that the prevalence of this kind of individualism is driving us apart. People today lead atomized, self-absorbed lives. We have retreated away from each other, into our homes, and into ourselves. While this negative concomitant of rampant individualism is sometimes openly recognized and its presence is regarded as less than ideal, the dominant culture has made peace with it. It is all seen as part of the march of progress—an inevitable consequence of economic development. The attitude seems to be: if the price to pay for individual freedom is social distance, then so be it.

Unfortunately, the individualism we have is of a deficient quality. Individualism should imply uniqueness, difference, originality among individuals; that is to say, it should imply *individuality*. The individualism of our day utterly fails in this regard. Social detachment has not been a boon for individuality. It seems, instead, to have secured the opposite outcome. Oddly enough, the age of individualism is also the age of conformity.

Mass production, if it is to be sustained, must be accompanied by mass consumption, and therein lies the source of our conformity. With the rise of the assembly line in the early twentieth century and the accompanying intensification of the production of consumer goods, "men and women," observes historian Stuart Ewen, "had to be habituated to respond to the demands of … productive machinery."[4] The status of conspicuous consumer, once reserved only for the wealthy, has been thrust upon everyone in industrialized nations and is working its way through the world as a whole. Our identities as family members, friends, students, workers, and citizens have come to be subordinated to consumerism.

Relationships between people are increasingly mediated with the help of commercial values. We go to school and work so that we can gather the means to partake in consumption. As for citizenship, when we think about participating in an effort to create societal reform, our minds first, and often only, consider the changes we can make in our consumption choices. The political sphere is rarely seen as worthy of engagement other than, of course, through token actions like voting and signing petitions.

According to the supporting narrative of the age of individualism, we should not be worried about the lack of serious engagement in the political sphere. Citizenship, in the strict sense of the word, is outdated. We are told that the market, which functions to satisfy individual wants, is much more democratic than any official political process could ever be. This "democracy" of consumption continuously grows in breadth and scope with the market, as those who are already conspicuous consumers increase their levels of consumption and formerly poor people join the new global middle class and become consumers. Everyone, goes the official narrative, can expect to be raised out of poverty and take part in the consumption frenzy. Oh, what a wonderful world it will be.

As we will discuss in the second chapter, our system of mass consumption relies on mass inequality and exploitation to function. It cannot be relied upon to meaningfully raise living standards for the underprivileged in our world. And as we will see in the third chapter, what a wonderfully unsustainable world it already is.

Claims about the democratic nature of our social system are the central focus of interrogation in this chapter. I hope to demonstrate to the reader that, in fact, the economic and political arrangements of our day are fiercely undemocratic. Rather than democracy (rule of the people) we have plutocracy (rule of the rich).

To start with, I ask how we can create a social system in which individuals may come to have individuality. I find that the answer lies in placing individual freedom atop a social foundation, which is in turn democratically constituted. I then take most of the rest of the chapter to examine various undemocratic aspects of our age. The discussion especially takes note of the nature of corporate power and the inability of a profit-oriented news media to create an informed citizenry. The chapter ends with a short discussion about how social activism, which seeks to change things for the better, is often too burdened by the strictures laid down by our age to create meaningful impact.

WHITHER INDIVIDUALITY?

The individual and society are often squared off against one another. We are told that we should be watchful of the value we give to society, lest it encroach upon individual liberty. There is perhaps some merit to this worry, but it should first be asked whether the individual and society have to be seen as necessarily opposed.

Margaret Thatcher, one of the leading advocates of modern-day individualism, once famously stated that "there is no such thing as society." According to this view, what we call society is simply a collection of individuals, while the individual is something of a self-sovereign, autonomous being. Any given society, thus, takes the form that it does because of the individuals that make it up. On the basis of such a perspective, it seems apparent that the individual deserves to be valued, while any claims that society makes on the individual need to be rebuffed. The individual should be left alone and not be burdened by obligations to support others.

This way of looking at the individual and society, however, is not consistent with reality.

An individual who is part of a society is who she is only because she is a part of that particular society. The individual becomes herself in large part through her interactions with others; she is a social creation. She has those who came before her and those who exist alongside her to thank for her identity. Language is perhaps the most easily identifiable feature of an individual's makeup that finds its source in historical and current social interaction. Only because others communicate through the use of spoken language can any individual do the same. In addition to language, the ideals we hold, how we perceive the world around us, the knowledge we have gained, the technology we use, and the careers we follow are in large part what they are because we are a part of a particular society.

Since the individual relies upon others for her development and she herself contributes to the development of other individuals, the individual and society do not appear to be necessarily opposed to each other. And social obligations do not seem to be outright insidious. Rather, it appears natural and necessary for individuals to have obligations to each other as well as to future generations.

At this point we are presented with a potentially frightening picture. If society can call upon the individual to fulfill social obligations, what is to become of individual freedom? To mediate this worry, we have to re-examine what freedom means. The age of individualism, as we have noted, anchors individual freedom upon the following principle: "You stay out of my way and I will stay out of yours." As a general rule, individuals should not inhibit each other's attempts to seek fulfillment, but this formulation of freedom as a standalone has the potential to be brazenly hostile to the concept of society. Just as the individual is a social creation, an accurate description of individual freedom must be firmly positioned on a social foundation.

It is perfectly fair to discuss freedom in terms of the ability an individual has to achieve fulfillment. It must be recognized, however, that society contributes to this freedom by doing quite a bit more than simply getting out of the way. Society helps to cultivate the desires the individual has and helps her to achieve these desires. If I enjoy playing soccer and not baseball, for example, it is likely that my feelings have been cultivated by the society in which I live and others around me likely feel the same way. In order to fulfill my desire to play soccer and improve my game, I will need regular access to a public field, and I will also need others to come along with me.

Moreover, our desire is often to seek not individual but collective fulfillment. I may desire to score a goal or two during a soccer match but a greater desire of mine will likely be for my team to win the match regardless of whether I am able to score.

Since society plays such an important role in helping individuals develop and achieve their desires, the concept of individual freedom cannot be thought of in individualistic terms. We need to work to structure society in ways that allow it to empower the individuals who are a part of it. We need to build a protagonistic society: one that seeks to enhance individual freedom by cultivating and helping to fulfill healthy physical, intellectual, and moral desires among individuals while discouraging the development and fulfillment of destructive desires.

It is not necessarily a violation of individual freedom for a society to lend itself to the fulfillment of certain desires over others. In fact, it should be clear that society cannot help but contribute to the cultivation of desires. Members of society can and should seek to create an environment in which individuals are protected from harm and are directed towards meaningful development. Just as a collective can cultivate an interest in soccer among individuals, it can cultivate an interest in rampant drug abuse among them; just as a collective can push individuals to become consumers, it can push them instead to become citizens; and just as a collective can encourage conformity, it can encourage individuality.

While it is clear that society has a mandate to actively shape the lives of the individuals who are a part of it, we do have to be wary of the very real dangers that have the potential to accompany this mandate. It is possible for individual freedom to be inhibited as a result of the active effort of a collective. Individuals can be taken advantage of, forced to give up their individuality and conform to a standard, or destroyed rather than developed. How are such circumstances to be avoided? To answer this question, we have to explore in detail what it is that makes a society.

Society, as we have come to see, is quite a bit more than the sum total of the individuals who make it up. It is something more complex, much more difficult to define. Perhaps one way to begin defining it is to say that society is a collective memory stretching back untold generations. This memory finds form in the lives of the individuals who make up society at any given time. But such a description on its own is perhaps better suited for the concept of culture, rather than society. It is too deterministic — the individual is not given the ability to contribute to and shape existing and future society. In other words, it does not present the individual as a conscious and assertive part of society. To take account of this essential element, we have to note that *society is community*. And a community can hardly exist among individuals who are not willful, engaged participants within it. As the philosopher John Dewey points out:

> Persons do not become a society by living in physical proximity, any more than a man ceases to be socially influenced by being so many feet or miles removed from others. A book or a letter may institute a more intimate association between human beings separated thousands of miles from each other than exists between dwellers under the same roof. Individuals do not even compose a social group because they all work for a common end. The parts of a machine work with a maximum of cooperativeness for a common result, but they do not form a community. If, however, they were all cognizant of the common end and all interested in it so that they regulate their specific activity in view of it, then they would form a community.[5]

To put it another way, a collective can only be considered a society if it is democratically constituted. Dewey notes that many aspects of our social arrangement cannot be described as societal: "Individuals use one another so as to get desired results, without reference to the emotional and intellectual disposition and consent of those used." Social inequality, in the many ways that it is manifested — in economic class, political office, place of birth, skin color, gender, as well as others — is what permits this abuse. We must seek to institute societal (democratic) relations into the workings of every kind of collective—whether it is the household, workplace, community, or nation—if we are to protect the individual from potential abuse.

It is impossible to avoid having the collective shape the lives of the individuals who make it up. The only way to ensure that individuals are not abused by the collective, but instead have their development and freedom expanded, is to have power be equally distributed among individuals. In such a group, the individuals actively shape the collective, which, in turn, shapes them. This is where true individual freedom is found. Society can direct and shape the development of individuals, not to create individuals who all think and behave alike, but to create a setting in which people are able to achieve the complete expression of their own individual personalities.

DEMOCRACY AND THE CORPORATION

How does the age of individualism live up to the democratic ideals we have laid out? Supporters of our social arrangement tell us that it does quite well. They point to the ascendance of the market as proof. The formal political institutions of our day, or any age, are largely undesirable, they say, because these institutions allow individuals to be vulnerable to collective abuse. Bureaucratic government is powerful and distant from common people. If allowed to become large and run rampant, it will intervene in the lives of individuals for its own advantage and consequently limit their development and freedom. As such, its reach and power should be minimized to the extent that is possible.

The process of collective decision-making can instead be largely left to the market, we are told. Here the wishes of individuals are not serviced according to the standards of a bureaucracy, but in the way individuals themselves want. All of their wants and needs can be settled without the troublesome involvement of powerful government. Described in this way, we are made to believe that the market is a democratic institution; the people rule themselves. This is a terribly false picture.

While the power concentrated in government is certainly something to be wary of, the same can be said about concentrated private power. Bureaucratic government can abuse individuals by mobilizing its political power. Moneyed interests can likewise orient society to service their own interests and abuse individuals by mobilizing their economic power. And what usually happens when calls to minimize the reach of government are followed is that the state ceases to function on behalf of individuals as a countervailing force against concentrated private power; it comes to be firmly captured by private power and becomes an even larger burden to individuals.

In any case, as matters currently stand, private power poses a larger danger to individual freedom than the state does. As Noam Chomsky points out, governments as they exist today are at least to some extent accountable to the public, whereas corporate power is almost perfectly unaccountable.[6] Chomsky contends that if we had to borrow a term from politics to describe the organizational form of corporations, the most fitting one would be "fascism." Within corporations

> power goes strictly top-down, from the board of directors to managers to lower managers and ultimately to the people on the shop floor, etc. There's no flow of power or planning from the bottom up. Ultimate power resides in the hands of investors, owners, banks, etc. People can disrupt, make suggestions, but the same is true of a slave society. People who aren't owners and investors have nothing much to say about it. They can choose to rent their labor to the corporation, or to purchase the commodities or services that it produces, or to find a place in the chain of command... [C]orporations are subject to some legal requirements and there is some limited degree of public control. There are taxes and so on. But corporations are more totalitarian than most institutions we call totalitarian in the political arena.[7]

The corporation expends a considerable amount of effort in trying to dress up its totalitarian nature. It presents itself as a "corporate citizen." It funds the little league team in your city and a tree planting project in Sierra Leone, both of which are prominently featured on its website. And it releases an annual report detailing its commitment to "corporate social responsibility." These sorts of things are often presented as if they are part of an exciting new development.

We are told that as consumers become increasingly interested in modern-day concerns about human rights and the environment, corporations are, in turn, being forced to become increasingly enlightened. There is nothing new about this, and it has hardly anything to do with enlightenment. It is simply a part of an effort meant to entrench internal loyalty and create a shiny public image. In his 1928 book *Propaganda*, the father of public relations, Edward Bernays, observes, "Business realizes that its relationship to the public is not confined to the manufacture and sale of a given product, but includes at the same time the selling of itself and of all those things for which it stands in the public mind."[8] He writes that the

> successful businessman ... has annual dinners that are a compendium of speeches, flags, bombast, stateliness, pseudo-democracy slightly tinged with paternalism. On occasion he doles out honors to employees ... But these are merely the side shows, the drums, of big business, by which it builds up an image of public service, and of honorary service. This is but one of the methods by which business stimulates loyal enthusiasms on the part of directors, the workers, the stockholders and the consumer public.[9]

The organizational form of the corporation is highly undemocratic. Since individuals spend such a large amount of their time working, a social system can hardly begin to be considered democratic if the workplace does not have a societal arrangement. The age of individualism tells us that engagement with any given actor in the marketplace is a matter of choice. This "freedom of choice" argument offers that if an individual dislikes the organizational form or behavior of any given corporation she can make the choice of refusing to engage with it by refusing to be employed by it, and abstaining from purchasing its products and services. Some corporations will invariably be more democratically structured than others, so why not just deal with those that are relatively good? Any individual can even decide, if she is so willing, to only engage with companies run as cooperatives, or start such a cooperative with others who are likeminded. If we were to follow this logic, we would have to believe that people must take jobs with corporations because they *freely* want to work under totalitarian circumstances instead of working in a cooperative setting.

To begin with, the "freedom of choice" argument conveniently fails to note that even most people in the industrialized world, to say nothing about poor countries, are not in a position to dictate anywhere near the full terms of their employment. Deciding not to seek employment with a corporation, and working instead for an existing cooperative or starting a new one, is a luxury choice not available to most of the people on the planet. Secondly, though many people may deem themselves to be perfectly content while working under dictatorial conditions, this can hardly serve as a justification for the existence of such workplaces. Many serfs living in feudal Europe may have likewise been satisfied with their lot. Far from providing justification for feudalism, this lends support to the bitter observation made by the main character in Fyodor Dostoyevsky's classic *Crime and Punishment*: "Man grows used to everything, the scoundrel!"[10]

Social circumstances, as we have noted, shape the expectations and desires that individuals come to hold. Having been conditioned with a certain set of expectations, individuals may be quite happy with meeting them. Just because serfs or lowly employees of corporations may be happy with what they have does not mean that they would *freely* choose such a circumstance. A democratically constituted social arrangement would, to be sure, inculcate higher expectations within individuals.

It is perhaps also important to point out that while people may become outwardly accustomed to the discipline of a hierarchical work environment, research shows that trouble continues to brew underneath the surface. It turns out that having a position near the bottom of the workplace ladder is bad for one's physical health. When researchers first started looking into the relationship between health and hierarchy, they expected to find that those at the very top, because of their higher levels of responsibility, would be the most likely victims of stress. What they actually found was the exact reverse. Those at the bottom experience an increased amount of stress because of lack of control over their work. This translates into, among other health problems, increased rates of heart disease.[11]

Finally, the "freedom of choice" argument ignores the fact that we are influenced by corporations regardless of our individual decisions in the marketplace. The size and scope of corporations mean that engagement with them is not based strictly on whether one chooses to buy what they are selling or to become employed by them. "Their power and effects," one pair of academics notes, "are almost incalculable—not only to the economy but also to politics, society, culture, and values."[12] The biggest corporations are economically larger than most of the countries on the planet. For instance, the oil giant ExxonMobil has a greater economic output than countries like Pakistan and New Zealand.[13]

Such massive amount of economic power does not sit idle and wait for individual consumers and workers to engage it. It intervenes forcefully into people's lives. It projects itself into commercial, public, and private spaces. It captures political power and influences policy-making. And it ends up shaping our cultural and physical environments in ways that create a dependency upon it.

Why is it, for instance, that so many of us own and drive cars? Walkable living environments, with good access to public transit for distant travel are healthier, more pleasant, and less polluting than communities that are comparatively more reliant on cars. Car-free travel also ends up being much cheaper for individual travelers and government budgets. In Japan, where walking and public transit function as good substitutes for cars, total spending on transportation amounts to 9 percent of the country's GDP.

By contrast, in the U.S., where living environments make car-free travel comparatively more difficult, total spending on transportation is 20 percent of GDP.[14]

Despite the obvious advantages of traveling without cars, public policies in the U.S. have for a long time incentivized the use of cars over other forms of travel. For example, under the U.S. tax code, employers are permitted to spend as much as $175 per month on parking for every employee that drives to work, but they can only spend up to $65 per employee for public transit. This parking subsidy results in an annual cost of $50 billion to taxpayers.[15]

But this is not the only parking taxpayers subsidize. In 2002 American taxpayers paid a subsidy of more than $100 billion for off-street parking.[16] Added to these incentives are subsidies for road construction and maintenance, tax breaks for car manufacturers, and city planning that makes living without a car all but impossible.

Our reliance on cars has obviously not come about as a result of thoughtful reflection and honest societal debate. It exists, rather, because of corporate power. Car manufacturers fund the campaigns of political candidates and furiously lobby various levels of government to obtain privileged treatment; they spread propaganda and shape our cultural values, going to the extent of giving away free classroom resources that carry their logos in the hope that these will create "imprint conditioning"[17]; and the largest car manufacturer, General Motors, has been found guilty of unlawfully conspiring to purchase streetcar lines for the express purpose of running them out of business.[18] If car manufacturers would just sit and wait for us to engage them as individual consumers and employees in the marketplace, we would live in quite a different world today.

SELFISHNESS GALORE

An argument that is sometimes raised in defense of corporations is that they should be seen as people because they are made up of people. Fascist governments are made up of people as well, but one never seems to hear the same reasoning being used to defend them. But if corporations were human beings, they would be completely cynical, anti-social individuals. Interestingly enough, the age of individualism would have us believe that this is actually what all human beings are like. Apparently we function, just as corporations do, to maximize our individual self-interest. We are told that even when individuals take actions to help others, they are really doing it to raise their social prestige and sense of self-worth. The age of individualism is thus said to have the support of human nature.

Often, evidence for the singularly self-interested nature of human beings is sought in evolutionary biology. Social Darwinism, the idea that human society functions on the basis of "survival of the fittest," is the outcome of this. To counter such thinking, the zoologist and anarchist-philosopher Peter Kropotkin showed in his book *Mutual Aid: A Factor of Evolution* that the evolutionary struggle makes itself apparent in more than just competition. In fact, one finds a great amount of "mutual aid" among individuals in any given species. In nature, those who can cooperate with each other will often have an easier time surviving and producing offspring than those who are unceasingly competitive. That is to say, the "fittest" are often those who can best work together. Therefore, if evolutionary biology is to be used as a guide, we would expect human society to be seen more as a cooperative undertaking than a competitive one-against-all struggle.

It is clear that humans have the ability to be both cooperative and competitive, to be compassionate as well as greedy. We are complex beings. Individuals often do act out of self-interest, but we may also behave in the way we do because we are feeling bored, or lazy, or angry, or happy, often against our better judgment. What is more, we often act out of genuine concern for others. The political economist Adam Smith, whose views and works are routinely abused by supporters of the age of individualism, certainly recognized this. *The Theory of Moral Sentiments*, his book on ethics, begins with the following passage:

> How selfish soever man may be supposed, there are evidently some principles in his nature, which interest him in the fortune of others, and render their happiness necessary to him, though he derives nothing from it except the pleasure of seeing it. Of this kind is pity or compassion, the emotion we feel for the misery of others, when we either see it, or are

made to conceive it in a very lively manner. That we often derive sorrow from the sorrows of others, is a matter of fact too obvious to require any instances to prove it; for this sentiment, like all the other original passions of human nature, is by no means confined to the virtuous or the humane, though they perhaps may feel it with the most exquisite sensibility. The greatest ruffian, the most hardened violator of the laws of society, is not altogether without it.[19]

A fundamental aspect of being human lies in our ability to judge between right and wrong, good and bad. In other words, we have an intrinsic moral sense. Naturally, this means that we have the ability to *act* based on the judgments we make. To suggest, therefore, that we are only capable of acting in our own self-interest is nothing less than the denial of our humanity. As it turns out, the way in which the market system works in compelling us to only consider our self-interest has dehumanizing effects. Getting caught up in the self-interest rat race brings us into conflict with our sense of morality. To try to put this conflict to rest, we are forced to seek rationalizations for our conduct. Rationalizations, including the idea that humans are only capable of acting out of self-interest, are conveniently provided by the propaganda systems that function on behalf of political and economic power. By taking up these rationalizations, we end up distorting a basic foundation of our humanity, our moral compass.

2 + 2 = 5

The most perverse of all rationalizations cultivated by the age of individualism tries to do away with our moral faculties altogether. In our brave new post-modern world, fanciful questions like "What is the truth, really?" abound. There is no such thing as truth, comes the answer. It is all a matter of perspective. Everything is subjective. Each individual has her own reality. My reality is different from yours. There is no right or wrong. What I believe to be right is right for me, and what you believe to be right is right for you. Truth and morality, as they are commonly thought of, are simply social constructs.

Individuals have become detached from their social surroundings to such an extent that the idea that we can each live in separate bubbles without needing to contend with a common reality sounds reasonable to us. For most practical purposes, of course, people do not seriously believe in the idea that there is no such thing as reality. If an engineer is designing a bridge, she makes sure to get her calculations right. Not "right" according to a supposed reality that is a figment of her imagination or a social construct, but right according to the laws of physics. And despite the talk about the virtues of moral relativism, it is not something that people are generally willing to live by. As the philosopher Peter Singer observes:

> If we see a person holding a cat's paws on an electric grill that is gradually heating up, and when we

vigorously object he says, "But it's fun, see how the cat squeals," we don't just say, "Oh, well, you are entitled to follow your own beliefs," and leave him alone.[20]

The idea that there is no such thing as truth has very real consequences, however, when people are dealing with seemingly distant matters. Politics is one such arena. The pervasiveness of the "everything is an interpretation" attitude leads to an ambivalent and apathetic political culture in which most citizens fail to develop thought-out convictions and ideals—"One person's terrorist is another person's freedom fighter"; "Some people believe that human-made climate change is happening, but others disagree." The truth can be distorted, disguised, or altogether flouted and barely anyone seems to mind because, well, everything is a matter of interpretation.

But in a world such as ours, where power is so unequally distributed, individuals do not get to believe whatever they want about matters of political significance, even if they want to believe nothing at all. They instead generally go along with what the powerful want them to believe. Indeed, as George Orwell notes, the idea that there is no such thing as truth is nothing less than the basis upon which totalitarianism is built:

> In the past people deliberately lied, or they unconsciously coloured what they wrote, or they struggled after the truth, well knowing that they must make many mistakes; but in each case they believed

that 'facts' existed and were more or less discover-
able. And in practice there was always a considerable body of fact which would have been agreed to
by almost everyone ... It is just this common basis
of agreement, with its implication that human beings are all one species of animal that totalitarianism destroys. Nazi theory indeed specifically denies
that such a thing as 'the truth' exists. There is, for
instance, no such thing as 'Science'. There is only
'German Science', 'Jewish Science', etc. The implied
objective of this line of thought is a nightmare world
in which the Leader, or some ruling clique, controls
not only the future but *the past*. If the Leader says of
such and such an event, 'It never happened'—well,
it never happened. If he says that two and two are
five—well, two and two are five.[21]

We do not, of course, live in a totalitarian nightmare, but
the tendency that Orwell points to is not altogether absent
from our world. If the ruling clique, for example, says
Saddam Hussein's Iraq has weapons of mass destruction
(WMDs) and it must be stopped from using them by being
subject to a military invasion, then that is the way things
go. It matters little that there exists no evidence to support
their claims.

In July 2002, top British government, defense, and intelligence personnel met to discuss the impending invasion of Iraq. The leaked summary of this meeting explicitly
states that "the intelligence and facts were being fixed" by

the U.S. government around the pre-determined goal of launching a war. Remarkably, the document, known as the Downing Street memo, has the following in its headline: "This record … should be shown only to those with a genuine need to know its contents."[22] It seems apparent that "those with a genuine need to know" that an illegal war is being planned include the people who are going to be the victims of it, those who will fight in it, those who will fund it, as well as all those who will have to witness their fellow human beings suffer and die just so that the whims of empire can be placated. All of us were not, however, included on the list of people officially allowed access to the document. The ruling clique reserved for us the "intelligence and facts" especially "fixed" for our consumption.

But how is it that the powerful can get people to believe their made up claims at a time when information supposedly flows freely and there exists a free press? Even before the invasion of Iraq commenced, long before the Downing Street memo was leaked in 2005, it was clear that "the intelligence and facts were being fixed." One hardly had to be a diligent observer to know that there existed no just case for war. And indeed, it is clear that many people did see matters as they were. Millions of people in some sixty countries around the world, including the United States, demonstrated against the war before it began. This was an unprecedented development. Never before in history had such massive demonstrations *preceded* a war.

Yet, at the time of the invasion in March 2003, according to a survey conducted by the Pew Research Center, more than 70 percent of the American public was in support of the war. This support expectedly declined over time as it was revealed that no WMDs were found, U.S. military casualties (there seems not to have been much concern for Iraqi civilian casualties) and the financial costs of the war mounted, details about detainee abuse at Abu Ghraib prison were made public, etc. In spite of all this, in early 2008 almost 40 percent of the American public was still supportive of the initial decision to invade Iraq.[23] What is more, according to a 2007 *Newsweek Magazine* poll, more than 40 percent of Americans believed that Saddam Hussein's regime had been involved in the World Trade Center attacks of September 11, 2001.[24]

Despite the fumbling insistence of the Bush administration that Saddam Hussein was allied with al-Qaeda, it has long been apparent that no such thing was the case. In the months preceding the invasion of Iraq, the U.S. intelligence community made it clear that links between the two were tenuous at best.[25] A year after the war began, the 9/11 Commission would conclusively report that although there had been occasional contact between al-Qaeda and Iraq since the mid-1990s, when Osama Bin Laden met with a senior Iraqi intelligence official in Sudan, "we have seen no evidence that these ... contacts ever developed into a collaborative operational relationship. Nor have we seen evidence indicating that Iraq cooperated with al-Qaeda in developing or carrying out any attacks against the United States."[26] Why then did so many Americans continue to believe that Saddam Hussein was involved in the 9/11 attacks? How could the population of the most powerful nation on the planet be so utterly misinformed?

A consideration of central importance to this discussion is that political democracy cannot exist where the people are ignorant about elementary truths about matters of political concern. It matters little that the "representatives" of the people are elected. If what is accepted as "truth" is heavily curtailed by those in charge of the political machinery, then it is not the people who rule, but the few.

THE AGE OF PROPAGANDA

In order to understand how it is that the people are so often misinformed, we must explore the nature of the news media, which is where most of the public's insight into matters of political significance comes from. By examining the news media in detail, we can see, among other things, some of the interconnections between concentrated political and economic power.

To begin on a general note, the *mass* media as a whole contributes a great deal to the formation of the political ideals and attitudes that people hold. Entertainment delivered by the mass media provides distractions that contribute to political apathy. In this, as Edward Herman and Noam Chomsky observe, the media serve the same function that the "games of the circus" did in ancient Rome. The circus of reality television, sensationalist music videos, and glorified violence helps to make it so that we are

just not really all that concerned about the difference between Osama Bin Laden and Saddam Hussein and all the
other people with strange sounding names. And when
the surveyor asks if someone named Saddam had something to do with the 9/11 attacks: "Well, yes, that sounds
about right."

The news media are not doing much to combat this political apathy. A significant amount of news ends up being
a part of, or about, the circus. Celebrity marriages and the
like receive an inordinate amount of coverage. When we
finally get to matters of political importance, the coverage
tends to be highly biased in favor of power.

Only five firms control most of the mass media in the
United States. The majority of the information and entertainment that the American public consumes through
television, radio, newspapers, magazines, books, and
films is brought to them by Time Warner, The Walt Dis-
ney Company, News Corporation, Viacom, and Bertelsmann.[27] These companies are massive. Their holdings
and operations span the globe. Accordingly, an overview
of the media also gives us insight into the workings of the
corporation.

Media conglomerates, like corporations in general, do
not engage with consumers on mutually agreed upon
terms. Given that they have overwhelmingly disproportionate amounts of power, they are able to set the stage in
their own favor. The firms that control the media actively
use their power to affect political outcomes. They engage,

as is common among corporations, in the rituals of lobbying and making large campaign contributions to political candidates. The ability to directly remit information to millions of people gives the firms that own the mass media an additional kind of power that the corporate world in general does not possess. Control of the media, as the pioneering media critic Ben Bagdikian notes, is itself political power: "The five dominant media firms ... have that power and use it to enhance the values preferred by the corporate world of which they are a part."[28]

The news media's propensity to champion certain values over others and their overall function of misinforming the public are most thoroughly explained and documented in Edward Herman and Noam Chomsky's *Manufacturing Consent*.[29] In their classic study, the authors develop a "propaganda model" to describe the way in which market-based news systems work. The model comprises a set of "filters" through which newsworthy information is sifted. A large amount of information does not make it through the filters. That which comes out tends to be propaganda on behalf of political and economic power. Herman and Chomsky's propaganda model is an unrivaled tool for coming to understand the nature of the news media. For this reason, it will be worthwhile to briefly discuss these filters and their implications. Doing so will lend support to not only the arguments that have been put forward in this chapter but also serve as a basis for important points raised later in the book.

The first filter in the model is concentration of owner-ship. Over time, media ownership has come to be held in an ever-smaller number of hands. This has happened in large part as a result of the advantages provided by econ-omies of scale, and political lobbying through which reg-ulations that restricted concentration of media ownership were eliminated. When Ben Bagdikian first published *The Media Monopoly* in 1983 a total of fifty firms controlled the majority of the media in the U.S. By the time the seventh edition of the book was published in 2004 only five firms, as noted earlier, owned most of the media in the country.

In addition to the Big Five media giants, there exist mas-sive conglomerates whose interests in the media only ac-count for one segment of their varied holdings. General Electric (GE) is the largest of these.[30] GE owns a 49 percent stake in NBC Universal, but also has interests in electrical power distribution, weapons manufacturing, oil, finance, healthcare, as well as a host of other industries. Concentra-tion of media ownership in the hands of large conglomer-ates makes it so that information that conflicts with the in-terests of the owners is sidelined, while perspectives that reflect the interests of the owners are hailed.

The second propaganda filter is the reliance of the me-dia on advertising as its primary source of revenue. Just as concentration of ownership results in the filtering out of news that the owners would rather not have broadcasted, stories and perspectives that clash with the world-view of advertisers have a hard time finding light, while informa-tion that supports their world-view makes it into the news

relayed to people with ease. As Bianca Mugyenyi and
Yves Engler document:

> In the early 1970s, controversy erupted as Congress
> deliberated on new safety standards. During this
> debate the *New York Times* ran stories that were, in
> the words of a former staff member, "more or less
> put together by the advertisers." *New York Times*
> publisher Arthur Ochs Sulzberger admitted that if
> the auto industry's position on safety and auto pol-
> lution were not presented, it "would affect the ad-
> vertising." As the source of nearly a fifth of newspa-
> per ad revenue, the automakers called in favours to
> successfully push back against seatbelt and airbag
> laws.[31]

The advertising filter also puts pressure on the media to
cater their news to upper-class audiences, who have the
wealth to purchase the goods and services being adver-
tised. As a result, perspectives that are sympathetic to the
poor and working classes are sifted out.

The third filter has to do with the way in which news
is sourced. Having journalists all over the place collecting
potentially newsworthy information would be extremely costly. It is much more economically efficient to place
correspondents in locations such as the White House and
Downing Street, where newsmakers reliably relay information to journalists. Corporate press releases and spokes-
persons are also dependable sources of information. This
reliance on government and corporate sources makes the

media unwilling to challenge the official accounts relayed to it, out of fear that upsetting powerful actors may result in the loss of privileged access to newsworthy information in the future.

The fourth filter has to do with what Herman and Chomsky refer to as "flak." If a media outlet runs a story that portrays the government or powerful private actors in a negative light, it can expect to generate a response—or flak. The response can take the form of complaints, petitions, as well as threats of, or actual, legal action. Flak can come from the entity directly wronged, as well as from corporate-funded media watchdog groups like Accuracy In Media. Dealing with flak increases costs for the media. Its prevalence conditions them to be wary of running stories that may elicit it.

Finally, there is the "anti-enemy" filter. It is an ideological perspective promoted by those in power. It characterizes the enemy entity as simply evil and lacking any rational basis for behaving in the way it does. In contrast, this filter regards "us" as altogether good. Our actions are directed towards fighting evil. It may be that we are sometimes forced to make difficult and tragic decisions while attempting to subdue the enemy. From time to time, we may even falter in the fight between good and evil. But the fundamentally good nature of our intentions cannot be challenged. The adoption of this perspective by the media results in the suspension of critical thought and judgment when recounting our crimes, and a willingness to exaggerate the crimes of the enemy.

Writing in the late 1980s during the Cold War, Herman and Chomsky named this filter "anti-Communism," but it can more generally be described in terms of fear and hatred of the official enemy, whoever that may be at any given time. Today, terrorism can be seamlessly substituted for yesterday's Communism. The authors, for instance, relate that as a result of this filter there came into being a "dichotomized world of Communist and anti-Communist powers."[32] George W. Bush, in a speech following the attacks of September 11, sought to erect a similarly dichotomized world order when he declared, "Either you are with us, or you are with the terrorists."[33]

Herman and Chomsky provide striking examples of how the news media functions as propaganda on behalf of power. They note, for instance, that the media tend to treat people wronged by enemy states as "worthy victims," while those wronged by friendly governments or their own government are accorded "unworthy" status. "Worthy victims" are given sympathetic treatment. Their victimizers are readily identified and unequivocally condemned. When it comes to "unworthy victims," however, understated language is used and rationalizations are provided. For example, both Turkey and Iraq have long victimized their minority Kurdish populations, but they have been given quite different treatment in the U.S. media.

Turkey has been a close U.S. ally while Saddam Hussein's Iraq had been an enemy state ever since the Gulf War of 1990–91. In a 1999 *New York Times* op-ed, U.S. diplomat Peter Galbraith offered that "while Turkey represses its own Kurds, its cooperation is essential to an American-led mission to protect Iraq's Kurds from renewed genocide at the hands of Saddam Hussein."[34] Herman and Chomsky counter, "Turkey's treatment of its Kurds was in no way less murderous than Iraq's treatment of Iraqi Kurds, but for Galbraith, Turkey only 'represses,' while Iraq engages in 'genocide.'"[35] The authors note that in the period of 1990-1999 the word "genocide" was used in reference to Iraq's treatment of Kurds 132 times by a set of five leading U.S. news publications, including the *New York Times* and the *Washington Post*. In contrast, during the same period these publications applied the word "genocide" to Turkey's treatment of Kurds only fourteen times.[36]

A more recent example illustrating the propaganda role of the media is found in a 2010 Harvard Kennedy School study that assesses the coverage given in the U.S. media to the practice of waterboarding, a form of torture in which a restrained captive is made to feel the sensation of drowning.[37] The researchers found "a significant and sudden shift in how newspapers characterized waterboarding" after it was revealed that the U.S. military was using the technique on prisoners captured in the so-called War on Terror. The *Los Angeles Times*, for instance, referred to or implied that waterboarding was torture in twenty-six out of twenty-seven articles written on the subject from the 1930s to the early 2000s. In comparison, during the period of 2002-2008 the *Times* referred to or implied that waterboarding was torture in only three out of sixty-three articles.[38]

The U.S. media's cheerful support for government policy is crucial in procuring public support for unlawful and
unjust government conduct. The corporate sector is, likewise, a beneficiary of the propaganda role of the media.
A vivid example of the support economic power receives
from the media is provided by the coverage given to protests against the likes of the World Trade Organization
and Wall Street. The media tend to seesaw between depicting protestors as either immature rioters or strangely
dressed hippies. What the protestors stand for is generally
ignored, and when their concerns are addressed they are
caricatured and belittled. Rarely do we see such demonstrations depicted as what they really are: attended overwhelmingly by peaceful protesters, many of whom have a
polished understanding of the issues at stake.

The media's reluctance to truthfully report on the building climate change crisis is another stark example of kow-
towing to corporate power. Human-made climate change
is an established fact. We know it is occurring and that it
poses a serious threat to our survival. The media do not
seem to be so certain, however. Coverage of climate change
routinely showcases "both sides" of the so-called debate
on whether climate change is real and caused by human
actions. As we will see in the third chapter, there is no such
debate within the scientific community. There has been
no such debate for a number of decades. By consistently
placing an ambiguous framing around the issue of climate
change, the media confuse the public and help to weaken
political resolve for reducing greenhouse gas emissions.

This is of great benefit to corporations who have made the destruction of the environment their business.

The media's propaganda role is not the result of what could be called a "conspiracy." Journalists and editors do not sit in boardrooms and discuss how they are going to misinform the public and provide support to the status quo. Rather, it is the institutional arrangement in which the media are based that leads to the production of propaganda. As Herman and Chomsky note, "Most biased choices in the media arise from the preselection of right-thinking people, internalized preconceptions, and the adaptation of personnel to the constraints of ownership, organization, market, and political power."[39]

The propaganda model does not predict that the media will behave as a rigid, uniform entity unwilling to engage in debate and dissent. Any press that is popularly accepted as "free," and regards itself as such, could not function upon a monolithic basis. There certainly exists debate within the media. What is more important, however, is the nature of the debate – specifically, the range of the difference in opinion. If the debate is constrained within strict enough limits, it can actually help to further entrench the status quo, rather than being a challenge to it. As Chomsky observes:

> The smart way to keep people passive and obedient is to strictly limit the spectrum of acceptable opinion, but allow very lively debate within that spectrum—even encourage the more critical and dissident

> views. That gives people the sense that there's free
> thinking going on, while all the time the presupposi-
> tions of the system are being reinforced by the limits
> put on the range of the debate.[40]

Every so often, there may be an instance of an actually critical opinion being expressed in the media, but such occur-
rences are clearly the exception. We saw, for instance, lively debate within the media about the Iraq War. Especially
as the war dragged on, there developed a steady chorus of
opposition to the official U.S. government position. However, the farthest the dissenting voices in the media were
willing to go was to deem the course of the war a "failure"
and the initial decision to invade Iraq a "mistake." The
war was actually a criminal rampage, a result of which is
that more than a million Iraqis lost their lives and millions
more have been displaced and had their livelihoods destroyed.[41] The media should have referred to it as such and
plainly called for those who carried it out to be put on trial.
To describe it as a "failure" and a "mistake" conveniently does away with questions of criminality and injustice,
helping to give support to the idea that, whatever the outcome, the intentions of the invaders were pure-hearted.

We also see that the media report on corporate wrong-
doing, but here too matters up for discussion are bound
within strict limits. When corporations break the law, the
media often do cover it, though not as diligently as many
of us may think. Still more importantly, while corporate
misconduct as narrowly defined by existing laws and elite

ethics may be reported on, the fundamentally unjust nature of our economic system is not up for serious debate.

It deserves to be pointed out that the U.S. news media are not unique in their propaganda role. Wherever there exist market-based, profit-oriented media systems, a propaganda model is valid. One of the Big Five U.S. media conglomerates, Bertelsmann, is based in Germany. It was recently uncovered that, despite the firm's claims to the contrary, it had collaborated extensively with the Nazi government. It printed nineteen million books during World War II, including ones that glorified Adolf Hitler and contained anti-Semitic propaganda. When this revelation came to light, it was not picked up by the German press. It was first only the Swiss press, followed by the U.S.-based independent magazine *The Nation*, that decided to cover it.[42]

India, observes Sainath, has "a politically free media, but [it is] imprisoned by profit ... We have fashion correspondents, we have glamour correspondents, we have society correspondents; Not a single newspaper or channel in this country has a correspondent working fulltime on poverty."[43] In a country that is home to one-third of all those who live in extreme poverty,[44] one might expect the press to consider the plight of the poor a rather major issue. Unfortunately, poverty is a depressing subject. Advertisers trying to sell products to wealthy and middle-class consumers need them to be in a "buying mood," which doom and gloom do not help to create.[45]

ENTER ACTIVISM

Given all of the doom and gloom that exists in our world, many people are moved to act to try and change things for the better. Social activism is as old as human history, and there continues to be great need for it today. Only when people stand up to confront injustice, make sacrifices, and work together to build a better world will conditions improve in any meaningful way. Unfortunately, activism today is often too burdened by the values that come with the age of individualism to contribute to substantive change.

The most common way in which people try to address the problems that they note around them is by making changes in their individual lifestyle choices, and encouraging others to do the same. By making changes in the way we live and becoming "conscious consumers," this trend suggests, we can make positive change in the world. Along with lowering our overall levels of consumption, we are encouraged to consume organic, fair trade–certified, and locally produced goods. We are told that this will be beneficial for the environment, farmers in poor countries, and our individual health and spiritual well-being.

"Be the change you want to see in the world" is a statement often invoked in support of lifestyle-centric activism. Although these words find themselves regularly attributed to the wise Mahatma, there is no documentary evidence that suggests that they are in fact Gandhi's.[46] Even if the statement could be attributed to Gandhi, however, it can easily be demonstrated that it was not meant to be a pre-scription for activism.

While it could certainly be said that Gandhi's lifestyle choices were a large part of who he was, he understood that simply adopting a minimalist lifestyle would not bring about the change he wanted to see in the world. Creating social change, Gandhi recognized, requires social struggle. In his autobiography, he exhibits keen awareness of the fact that an individual on her own cannot make a difference. He gives special attention to organizing. For instance, while studying for the bar in London, Gandhi started a vegetarian club in the community in which he was living. He writes that "this brief and modest experience gave me some little training in organizing and conducting institutions."[47] He talks about sending telegrams, writing and printing literature, and touring; he documents his first meek attempts, and eventual improvement, in giving speeches to gatherings of people; he offers advice on managing the finances of social organizations; and throughout he stresses the need for "agitation."

Agitation is hardly possible within the marketplace through individual consumer action. We are asked to "vote with our wallets." The demand we generate will, over time, supposedly cause producers to offer more and more ethical products. Such entreaties misleadingly utilize language popularly associated with democracy to talk about an area of life that is fundamentally undemocratic. In the marketplace, some people have bigger wallets than others, and hence, there is an unequal distribution of "votes" among consumers; but perhaps more importantly, producers are not accountable to consumers in any way that resembles democratic institutions. Consumer sovereignty, the idea that independently derived consumer demand drives production, is inconsistent with reality.

In *Looking Backward*, an 1887 novel by Edward Bellamy, the main character makes his way to a utopian future where the profit motive no longer exists. He surmises that the new arrangement must save "a prodigious amount of lying," explaining to an acquaintance from the future that "when one's livelihood and that of his wife and babies depended on the amount of goods he could dispose of, the temptation to deceive the customer—or let him deceive himself—was wellnigh overwhelming."[48]

There is a word we use to refer to this kind of "lying" and efforts to "deceive the customer": marketing. Producers are vastly more powerful in comparison to consumers. A tremendous amount of effort is expended in order to convince consumers to purchase goods and services. In 2010, global spending on advertising amounted to more than $500 billion.[49] The process of production is strongly tied to the process of marketing of what is produced. Producers bring into existence a large part of the demand that they then fulfill. Writing on the "myth of consumer sovereignty," the economist John Kenneth Galbraith asks whether "a new breakfast cereal or detergent [is] so much wanted if so much must be spent to compel in the consumer the sense of want?"[50]

Justice, unfortunately, is not something that comes in commodity form. Campaigns focused on ethical consumerism have managed to achieve as much success as they can hope to find: niche markets have been created for especially conscious and wealthy consumers. Strategic uses of boycotts and other consumption-based initiatives as part of wider campaigns can help bring about progress in certain circumstances, but they have to be part of a bigger vision of change to matter.

On its own, there are many good things to be said about cutting back on what we consume and living in a way that is not grounded in petty materialistic values. Living a clutter-free life is a wonderful thing, but it is not in itself the same thing as working to create social change. Indeed, it should be recognized that those who have the ability to make token changes in their lives while retaining, or even enhancing, their standard of living can only do so because of their position as a privileged minority in a system that overtaxes the environment and exploits the poor. We cannot simply look inwardly and change our individual consumption choices while continuing to benefit from the overall social arrangement.

When faced with the kind of critique presented here, lifestyle-centric activists often counter that conscious consumerism is a good "first step." In my experience, however, those who endorse the idea that better consumption is a form of activism have a hard time moving on to anything else. Year after year I have seen those engaged in promoting lifestyle changes remain stuck in place. Their object has become to convince more and more individuals to become vegetarians, purchase fair-trade coffee, carpool to work, etc. And for most of those who sign on to this approach, the only "next step" they seem inclined to take is to intensify their engagement with conscious consumerism—finding endlessly greater ways to reduce their individual carbon footprint, compost and recycle, eat less meat, etc.

It seems to me that there is a qualitative difference between, on the one hand, embracing the individualism that defines lifestyle-centric activism and, on the other, coming to recognize the social dimensions of the problems we face. The former is not a bridge to the latter, but a distraction away from it. It is a step in the wrong direction. If anything, the first step to take in engaging with social activism should be to openly reject individualist approaches.

Having said all that, it is perhaps important to make the point that while making individual lifestyle changes may not be a form of activism in itself, making certain changes in the way we live can help us to better engage in activism. If we mean to be effective activists, the way we lead our lives will certainly have to differ from the norm. Anticlimactic though this suggestion may seem, the changes we should be most interested in making are those that will help give us space and time *to think*. It is easy enough to see that many of the routines of modern life conspire against thought and reflection. We are constantly bombarded with stimuli that overpower our senses. Things have gotten to the point where each of us carries around electronic devices that allow us to design the chronic sensory-overload we will be subjected to according to our own individual desires.

When we go out for a jog, we pop in our earphones and blast some tunes. While riding on the bus, we use our cellphones to text our friends or review the latest activity on a social media website. In class, we distract ourselves by playing video games on our tablet computers. At work we are unable to stop ourselves from checking if we received any new emails in the past fifteen minutes. From the time we wake up in the morning to when we go to sleep (usually very late because we are up watching the latest episodes of our favorite TV shows) we are fixated on one or another kind of external stimulus that keeps us out of touch with the thoughts inside our heads. This means that we lack the breathing room necessary to reflect on the state of the world, which has obvious consequences when it comes time to act in meaningful ways to change the way things are.[51]

But in rejecting a lifestyle that makes it difficult for us to think, we have to go beyond minimizing our reliance on electronic devices like music players and cellphones. We also have to see to it that we are not taking shortcuts when trying to gain an understanding of how the world works. YouTube, TED Talk[52] videos, and podcasts have of late become major sources of learning for activists. Taken on its own, this development may not necessarily appear to be anything to worry about. However, when it is considered alongside the fact that these sources have been adopted to the neglect of reading, it becomes clear that there is reason to be concerned.[53] The audio-visual format is a passive way to learn; plopping oneself in front of a screen and being fed information requires a lot less active engagement than slowly making one's way through a book. Though, of course, in our fast and impatient world even when we do get around to reading we hardly ever go about it in anything resembling an unhurried and meticulous fashion.

A serious commitment to activism requires us to establish a close relationship with the written word. A book not only provides a much more thorough account of its subject matter than an audio-visual source can, but literacy should be seen as a vital part of democracy. The practice of democracy—of people managing their collective affairs— must in large part be founded upon communication. And reading and writing, though they are lonely activities in the immediate sense, happen to be the most comprehensive forms of communication available to us.

Instead of creating "liberated spaces" in which activists come together to share in a minimalist livelihood, we need to create spaces in which we are encouraged to read and write, to learn, to discuss, to think. Rather than helping, action without thought and proper understanding can make things worse than they already are. And lifestyle-centric activism is certainly harmful. It feeds into the supporting narrative of our age by accepting the idea that supposedly autonomous individuals are to blame for our problems. Moreover, it gives a free pass to the powerful interests for whose benefit our social system operates.

The likes of ExxonMobil and General Motors are no doubt delighted to see activists focusing on the choices made by individual consumers while overlooking the ceaseless efforts corporations take to set the stakes in their favor. Charity, as we will see in the next chapter, is quite a bit like lifestyle-centric activism: it is rooted in the individualist impulse promoted by our age and it helps to conceal the social dimensions of the problems it seeks to solve.

If we intend to change the world for the better, instead of thinking of ourselves as consumers or donors, we must see ourselves as citizens. In contrast to the first two identities, which trend towards individualism and detract from political engagement, citizenship is an inherently collective and political occupation. It involves engaging in cooperative efforts to shape the world in which we live. While giving money to causes we believe in is important, it cannot stand alone as an adequate replacement for active involvement. We need to be involved.

But what do we do as activists who take a collective approach to activism? This path, unfortunately, is not inherently free from pitfalls. It is certainly possible, and often ends up being the case, that a collective approach is taken merely to propagate the values of the age of individualism. This happens when activists fail to consider that the solutions to the problems we face cannot be found while remaining within the bounds of the existing social arrangement, or when they go still further to accept the myths of our age and expressly endorse the institution of the market as a savior. The discussion in this chapter has tried to show that many of the ostensible merits of the market system are illusory. The following chapters build on this discussion by seeking to reveal that the market bears primary responsibility for creating the problems of global inequality and climate change, and there exists little scope that it can function as a cure for them.

We need to take up a collective approach to activism in a way that challenges the dictums of our age. We need to undermine institutions that encourage individualism and build society. That is to say, we need to work together to improve existing, and create new, accountable democratic institutions. Not only do we need to enhance the limited democracy that currently exists in the political sphere, we must democratize the economic sphere of life. Improved levels of democratization will help us to create an arrangement that is not based upon ever-increasing levels of production and consumption—a routine that is not only morally depraved on its own terms, but is also physically impossible to sustain. Curbing overconsumption and overproduction will, in turn, help bring an end to the exploitation of the poor and the destruction of the environment. Increased engagement with democratic institutions will also, of course, allow us to directly counter the exploitation of the poor and environmental destruction by reversing harmful policies and putting in place helpful ones. A more detailed discussion of this approach to activism will be offered in the final chapter.

For some reason, activists more than most others are prone to adopting ideas to do with moral relativism and the supposed subjective nature of reality. This kind of thinking is a great burden on our work. It makes us unwilling to search out the truth, develop strong convictions, and confront those responsible for making the world an unpleasant place.

"There is a reality out there," David Harvey points out, "and it is catching up with us fast."[54] Since the search for the truth is so important to our work, and since activists so often fail to take part in this search, the next two chapters are in large part devoted to exploring the sordid reality that we must face.

CHAPTER 2

Inequality and Activism

*True compassion is more than flinging a coin
to a beggar. It comes to see that an edifice which
produces beggars needs restructuring.*

—Martin Luther King, Jr.[1]

Charity … is the opium of the privileged.

—Chinua Achebe[2]

Alongside the tremendous poverty that exists in the world there also exists a tremendous amount of wealth, and global inequality often serves as an impetus for activism. The well-to-do are implored to use their privilege to relieve the suffering of the impoverished instead of, or at least in addition to, squandering their wealth and time on luxuries. Such appeals seem to have limited effect if one judges their success, as one should, based on the amount of poverty and anguish that remains in place even as the world is awash with ever-greater wealth. Since the close of the colonial era, the gap between the richest and poorest countries has expanded from 35:1 to almost 80:1. Today, the richest 200 individuals in the world have a combined wealth greater than that of the poorest 3.5 billion.[3]

This chapter explores a number of moral and practical questions that pertain to inequality. To begin with, it is worth asking whether those who are wealthy have any moral obligation to assist those who are in need. If they have no such obligation, then perhaps it could be said that the existing state of affairs, though it may not appear to be wonderful, has a right to persist. On the other hand, if the well-to-do have a responsibility to assist the less well-off, then we need to find ways to realize the obligation.

Based on intuition, most people would likely take the position that those who are wealthy do have a responsibility to assist the poor. For those few who may need convincing before they accept intuitive feelings, the Australian philosopher Peter Singer provides a straightforward line of reasoning in his widely read book *The Life You Can Save*.[4] Singer begins by making the case that if a person on her way to work walks by a shallow pond in which a child is drowning and no one else is in sight we would expect her to wade in and rescue the child. If she forwent rescuing the child and explained it away by saying that she did not want to spoil her shoes and be late for work as a result of having to go home to change, she would readily be identified as an immoral person.

Building on this scenario, Singer goes on to argue that those of us who have the means to assist people in extreme poverty have a moral responsibility to do so. Just as we would be expected to make the relatively small sacrifice of wading into a shallow pond to save a child, we should be expected to make comparatively small sacrifices to save, and positively alter, the lives of people who lack basic necessities. If ignoring a child drowning in a pond is immoral, not helping the impoverished when we are clearly in a position to do so is immoral as well.

Singer does not propose an exact threshold for when helping the less well-off becomes a responsibility. Rather, he suggests that the well-to-do should consider themselves morally obligated to help if they can "prevent something bad from happening, without sacrificing anything nearly as important."[5] What one considers to be "nearly as important" as something else may be open to some debate, but most things can be valued in relation to others without controversy. New shoes and the pay lost as a result of missing an hour of work, for instance, are nowhere near as important as a child's life.

The wealthy do have a strong moral obligation to assist the poor. But how should this obligation be carried out? According to Singer, the approach to take is to give charitable donations to organizations that conduct humanitarian efforts and development projects in poor countries. He asks that we consider giving up needless luxuries like bottled water, fashionable clothing, lavish meals, expensive cars, and extravagant vacations and instead regularly practice charitable giving. Singer recommends against taking on political campaigns in order to address the issue of poverty, pointing out that these are difficult to carry out and are prone to failure. Resources can be spent, he argues, in the arena of aid with much more assurance that the poor will be better off. Aid organizations directly save and improve lives by making available provisions such as mosquito nets and basic health care services. Singer estimates that a life can be saved in the developing world for the cost of anywhere from a few hundred to a few thousand dollars, depending upon the type of assistance delivered. Thus, if an individual adopts an austere lifestyle and gives regularly to aid organizations, she can be sure that she is making the world a better place.

Unfortunately, the approach Singer advocates is unsatisfactory, from both practical and moral standpoints. First, aid is an insufficient tool for helping the poor. The nature of the aid sector makes it difficult for the actors within it to directly assist those they seek to help. Even if aid could adequately do the job of directly helping poor people, however, it can only address the symptoms of poverty. It does not help to change the structural causes that bring poverty into being. Second, charitable giving gives rise to important moral questions that Singer fails to properly explore. Present-day wealth and poverty do not exist independently of one another; rather, one supports the other. Given this circumstance the moral thing to do, before considering any talk of charity, would be to undo the insidious connection between wealth and poverty. In addition, as a result of charitable giving, the social regard and self-esteem of the recipient is diminished, while that of the donor is raised. This feature of charity should also force us to question whether charity is the most moral response to inequality, especially considering the relationship between wealth and poverty noted above.

Peter Singer's *The Life You Can Save* has come to be embraced with some vigor by many who work in the aid sector as it contains a wide range of arguments that help the sector keep its happy self-image secure. For this reason, I have decided to use much of this chapter to offer a critique of many of the arguments put forward in the book.

INADEQUACIES OF AID

Aid is often given for political, rather than altruistic, reasons. Along with helping to provide cover for all the wrong the rich countries have done and continue to do, aid helps to procure support for the foreign policy objectives of donor countries. Aid given by multilateral institutions such as the World Bank is not considerably different. These institutions are, on the whole, funded and controlled by rich countries and operate for their benefit. Singer acknowledges that much of the aid rich countries give is meant "to serve political aims rather than to help the extremely poor."[6] He avoids thoroughly dealing with this uncomfortable reality, however, by insisting that we care not so much about what our governments do, but what we do as individuals. He wants individuals to give donations to non-governmental organizations (NGOs) that directly assist the poor. But even here the picture is not very rosy.

NGOs are not exactly the magnanimous do-gooders most of us imagine them to be. To begin with, they are often conceited in outlook and lack the willingness to coordinate with others. An El Salvadorian government official lamented that "If I invite 30 NGOs to help me in a decision, I'll have 30 different suggestions and one big fight."[7] The reason for the lack of comradeship among development NGOs can be traced to the fact that these organizations compete with each other to raise money. Thus, they are forced to resort to keeping distance between themselves, with each styling itself as different from the rest. Despite the variance in styling, the substance ends up being very similar. One expectedly finds that the ideological perspective adopted by NGOs is shaped by their sources of funding, which in significant part comprise Western governments. One outcome of this is that even though NGOs are popularly considered to be politically progressive, they can often be found parroting reactionary catchphrases such as "handouts don't work" (discussed in more detail below) and conducting their operations accordingly.

Broadly speaking, rather than being the vigilant defenders of the interests of the poor, NGOs tend to be meek, conformist organizations that fear treading on the toes of existing and potential donors, as well as other powerful actors. They fit themselves into small niches, steering clear of confrontation with structural realities and specific thorny issues. This has helped to create a state of affairs within the so-called development community where, as Denis Goulet notes, "primary emphasis in discussions is given to *aid*, which is but a single facet of a much larger issue, *development*."[8] Aid is a safe topic, whereas topics such as exploitation, both historical and contemporary, are not.

Western governments, through their respective aid agencies, tend to be large donors of NGOs, which should bring the latter's "non-governmental" bona fides into question. NGOs are handy instruments for promoting the interests of rich governments. For instance, soon after the U.S.-led invasion of Afghanistan was launched in October 2001, development NGOs were given a decisive part to play in the imperial escapade. Since codified in former-Secretary of State Hillary Clinton's so-called smart power doctrine, the role of NGOs has been to bring in the rear part of the "three Ds" strategy: "defence, diplomacy, and development."[9]

Through the use of "defence" the occupying troops capture and secure an area. "Diplomacy" is then engaged in to install pliable warlords in power. Finally, NGOs settle down to work with communities still reeling from conflict to promote "development." That an illegal[10] and unjust war is ravaging Afghanistan, and that their involvement provides legitimacy to the cause of the imperialists, appears to matter little to most NGOs working in the country. For imperialism, NGOs are the sometimes cheerleading, sometimes less cheerful but still acquiescent, missionaries of our time. In fact, the world of the NGO as it exists today finds its roots in a less overtly vulgar, yet no less destructive, imperialist project: the "structural adjustment" of the Third World. Beginning in the 1980s as governments in poor countries were forced to cut back on social spending in order to more securely service foreign debts, NGOs were brought in to ease the pain of the adjustment and provide legitimacy to the scheme. During the last three decades, as governments have been forced into retreat, NGOs have thrived.[11] For imperialism, NGOs are the sometimes cheerleading, sometimes less cheerful but still acquiescent, missionaries of our time.

For meaningful development and poverty reduction to take place, coordinated measures that are a part of a long-term vision must be adopted. Coming up with and implementing such visions are tasks that states, not NGOs, are in a position to perform. In fact, NGOs often undermine attempts by states to establish firm grounding. They create networks for the provision of health care, water, and other goods and services, undercutting efforts by states to coordinate such provisioning. It also happens that international NGOs usually pay much higher wages than the governments of poor countries are able to afford and can end up poaching away talented people who could be working for the public sector.

A state can only achieve competency in providing for its citizens if, among other things, it is given a chance to develop its capacity through trial and error. This takes time. Ineptness and corruption become less rampant as the state engages its citizens and the citizens, in turn, pressure the state to become more responsible. Where NGOs proliferate they can get in the way of this process of engagement between the state and citizens.

NGOs can often be found employing creative self-delusion in order to conceal the gap between the outcomes of their behavior and their stated objectives. Writing about NGOs in the U.K. Tina Wallace notes that "the argument of some NGOs, seeking to increase both their funding and their influence, is that taking money from the EU or DFID [the U.K.'s Department for International Development] allows a relationship and a dialogue to develop. They rarely analyze the reverse process, and ask how this relationship shapes and influences them."[12] On the basis of the same reasoning, Engineers Without Borders Canada (EWB), an organization I have volunteered with for several years, accepts large amounts of money from oil and mining companies.

The resource extraction sector has played a decidedly harmful role in poor countries. Interference in political affairs, tax evasion, environmental destruction, as well as labor and human rights violations are the regular companions of oil and mining companies in the developing world.[13] As Canada is home to two-thirds of all publicly traded mining companies, Canadian activists have a particular obligation to confront the injustices produced by the sector. EWB claims that taking money from such ill-famed actors allows the organization to be in a position to persuade them to change their behavior for the better. This is, of course, an absolutely absurd prospect.

Attention is not often given to the very real influence going in the other direction. Oil and mining companies donate money to organizations like EWB in order to bribe potential critics to become, or remain, quiet. By this standard, EWB has performed quite well. For instance, a 2010 bill in the Canadian Parliament that sought to impose slightly tougher regulations on the resource extraction sector received no support from EWB. The bill was closely contested (following intense lobbying from industry, it failed to pass by only six votes)[14] and certainly would have benefited from the support of an organization with the outreach capacity of EWB. While it was ignoring developments in the extractives sector, EWB was busy doing such world-changing things as promoting the purchase of fair-trade coffee.

We can be certain that the emancipation of the wretched of our world will not be brought about by the work of NGOs. This is not to suggest that there are no NGOs in existence that engage with issues of social justice valiantly. These, however, are the exception. The predicament that NGOs find themselves in is similar to that described by Edward Herman and Noam Chomsky's media propaganda model: there exists a system of incentives and constraints that force NGOs to adopt an outlook and behave in ways that benefit the powerful.[15]

In any case, it can justifiably be argued that even the work of those NGOs who are not particularly valiant can still result in directly changing people's lives. There are certainly plenty of examples of aid benefitting the poor.

But even when aid does work, it addresses the symptoms of poverty and not its causes. Worse, it diverts attention away from the causes. This feature of charity greatly diminishes its value as a tool for change and progress.

A large amount of hoopla surrounds the concept of charitable giving, which helps to promote the idea that if we donate money regularly we are "doing our part." We feel we can forgo learning about, and engaging more firmly, with matters of social justice. As a result, we fail to take up our duty as citizens who are working to collectively shape the world around us. Moreover, by seeming to lessen, or actually lessening to some degree, the pain of those wronged by the existing social arrangement, charity creates the false impression that structural change is not necessary.

Singer brings up the issue of the structural causes of poverty and aid potentially taking attention away from them, but only to quickly brush it aside. According to him, changing the existing social order is too tall a task. He writes that "there is little chance" that a "revolution" will come, hence we "need to look around for a strategy with better prospects of actually helping some poor people." But forget revolution; Singer seems to be opposed to fighting for political change of any sort. He uses the example of the 2008 Farm Bill in the U.S. to explain why. Despite the fact that there existed widespread opposition to the bill—not only anti-poverty campaigners but mainstream economists were also against it—it was passed by the U.S. Congress. "Defeats like this," writes Singer, "suggest that our efforts are better spent elsewhere, where we can be confident of making a difference."[16] If the abolitionists had adopted Singer's reasoning they would have focused on making immediate improvements in the living conditions of slaves instead of carrying out the more difficult fight to end slavery altogether.

Singer does have some critical things to say about NGOs. His main concern is that their work is not well monitored and evaluated, by themselves or others. Consequently, instead of providing facts about the effectiveness of their work, they are prone to using marketing tricks to promote themselves. He suggests that in order to introduce more accountability into the picture, NGOs must be incentivized and pressured to track and provide details about their work. One way to do this, Singer seems to suggest, is to increase the number and capacity of organizations that rate NGOs by the quality of work they do.[17] He fails to realize that for the aid sector to become accountable to the extent that is necessary would require a veritable revolution.

Not only are NGOs themselves inclined to resist becoming more accountable, as doing so would make raising money more difficult, but powerful interests such as rich governments and corporations who rely on NGOs to forward their agendas would also be against changing the status quo. Given that aid, to begin with, is not a useful means for creating lasting change, a revolution in the accountability of NGOs would not be particularly valuable. If we are going to devote effort to bringing about a revolution, it makes sense to do so in an arena where it will be of more consequence.

THE ORIGINS OF INEQUALITY

How did the world get to be such a horribly unequal place, and why does it remain so? It is generally thought that the existing global inequality is the result of some parts of the world becoming rich thanks to hard work and innovation, while most places have stayed as poor as they ever were. Poverty continues to reign throughout most of the planet, it is further supposed, despite the efforts of the rich world to assist those who are poor. And so the development economist Paul Collier writes that "poverty is simply the default option when economies malfunction."[18] Of course, this is complete hogwash.

Poverty is not a "default option" triggered because of an unfortunate "malfunction." Poverty as it exists today has been actively created through the historical process of capitalist development. The existence of global inequality supports the functioning of our economic system. It helps to keep in place the international division of labor so necessary to the existing production and consumption regime.[19] Who would work for a pittance to make sneakers for consumers in rich countries, for instance, if the impoverished masses of the Third World were to achieve a tolerable standard of living?

To chase the origins of the existing inequality to its historical roots one has to explore how the Third World was incorporated into the global capitalist order by way of colonization. The breakup of pre-capitalist relations, and the imposition of capitalist ones in their place, is symbolized in Chinua Achebe's novel *Things Fall Apart* in a powerful scene foretelling the arrival of the colonists:

> And at last the locusts did descend. They settled on every tree and on every blade of grass; they settled on the roofs and covered the bare ground. Mighty tree branches broke away under them, and the whole country became the brown-earth color of the vast, hungry swarm.[20]

The use of locusts to represent colonizers turns out to be especially fitting because of the historical association of these creatures with famine and hunger. The political economist Karl Polanyi explains that pre-capitalist communal social arrangement were characterized everywhere by "the absence of the threat of individual starvation." Imposing capitalist relations meant "the white man's initial contribution to the black man's world mainly consisted in introducing him to the uses of the scourge of hunger."

It was "only the penalty of starvation, not also the allurement of high wages," that made it possible to institute the market system. Without the threat of starvation, colonized peoples, as with pre-capitalist European populations before them, would not condescend to partaking in wage labor. "Thus," writes Polanyi, "the colonists may decide to cut the breadfruit trees down in order to create an artificial food scarcity or may impose a hut tax on the native to force him to barter away his labor."[21]

The forced incorporation of colonized societies into the world market made them vulnerable to its shocks and greatly multiplied food insecurity. The fact that communal livelihoods and traditional cultural institutions had been destroyed in the process of incorporation only heightened the vulnerability. The resulting famines that afflicted much of the colonized world caused indescribable destruction. In India alone, as Mike Davis details in *Late Victorian Holocausts*, millions died of hunger.[22] Many more were pushed into stunting poverty. The story elsewhere in Asia, Africa, and South America was similarly distressing.

Though the people of the Third World have successfully thrown off the colonial yoke, the strictures of global capitalism continue to confine them to an inferior position. There has been noticeable improvement in the overall living standards of many poor countries since the end of the colonial period, but the fundamental features of the international division of labor created during that time remain in force. The world remains an unequal place because of the needs of capitalism.

Certain people are privileged and others underprivileged. Much more than the work we put in, the amount of privilege we have determines the reward we obtain for our efforts. In fact, if we disregard causation, the relationship between effort put in and wealth acquired seems to be, if anything, inversely proportional. Those who are the least privileged are forced to work the hardest, and they receive the least reward.

As one learns to expect, the language we use to disguise the exploitation of the poor is eerily Orwellian: "free trade," "free enterprise," "freedom of contract." How much free-dom does a Bangladeshi sweatshop worker have? She can either engage in a contract with her employer or she can starve to death. This does not seem like freedom at all. In-deed, it appears to be very much like slavery. What we have, then, is a "slavery of contract." An enterprise built on the basis of such contracts is a "slave enterprise." And trade conducted among such enterprises is "slave trade."

Given the existing global social arrangement, charity should be seen as an immoral response to poverty. To borrow Singer's example, I should not push a child into a pond in which he will struggle to stay afloat, help to come up for air when I walk by once in a while, and act as if I am doing him a favor. I should, instead, stop pushing children into ponds. Likewise, those who benefit from the exploitation of others have a duty, first and foremost, to stop the ongoing exploitation. Simultaneously playing the roles of oppressor and savior is unbecoming—though, this is a age-old custom.

Charity and charitable rhetoric are commonly employed to conceal injustice. Our colonization of your land will result in your advancement, oppressors pronounce; our bombs will bring you democracy and women's rights; etc. Oppressors expend large amounts of effort in doling out kind words and aid money at heavily publicized occasions. When, inevitably, the results fail to match the high-mind-ed pronouncements, those on the receiving end of charity (and bombs, economic exploitation, etc.) are themselves blamed for their misery.

SOMALIA: A CASE STUDY

A July 21, 2011 editorial in the *Vancouver Sun* urged people to give donations in support of famine victims in East Africa. In a concessionary tone, the editorial notes that "we are… wary of appeals from a region where aid often appears to be poured into a bottomless pit and people seem no better off for it." It then immediately goes on to offer a response to the concession: "We must not let this weariness blind us to the human crisis that is now unfolding in a region that has known more than its share of misery. We must not let our disgust for leaders who create hardships for their own citizens or our attention to the pressing concerns of our daily lives distract us from the opportunity we now have to help."[23] The paternalism given voice to in the editorial closely echoes Rudyard Kipling's infamous 1899 poem, "The White Man's Burden":

> Take up the White Man's burden–
> The savage wars of peace–
> Fill full the mouth of Famine
> And bid the sickness cease;
> And when your goal is nearest
> The end for others sought,
> Watch sloth and heathen Folly
> Bring all your hopes to nought.

There apparently exists "a bottomless pit" into which our thankless mercy is being poured. The line about "leaders who create hardships for their own citizens" is no doubt a reference to the Somali militant group al-Shabab,[24] which has ties to al-Qaeda and, among having committed various other notorious acts, made efforts to block relief aid from being accessed by victims of the famine.[25] While al-Shabab are no doubt a loathsome bunch, it is noteworthy that the article fails to mention how they came to dominate the scene in much of Somalia. A look at recent Somali history quickly makes clear that responsibility for the influence attained by al-Shabab, as well as the broken-down state of Somalia in general, lies squarely with the West.

During the 1980s, the U.S. gave hundreds of millions of dollars in military and economic aid to the brutal regime of Somali dictator Siad Barre, supporting him as a counterweight against Soviet-allied Ethiopia. Barre's tyrannical rule inevitably led to growing opposition, the repression of which fuelled an armed rebellion against his government. A 1990 Human Rights Watch report notes that in an effort to crush the rebel uprising, Barre's "army turned its firepower, including its air force and artillery, against the civilian population ... On the claim of looking for [rebel] fighters and weapons, systematic house-to-house searches were carried out and thousands were shot in their homes." Artillery fire was directed at cities and "a substantial number of people died as their homes collapsed on them."[26] The report goes on to relate that President George H. W. Bush's administration "has refrained from publicly condemning the Siad Barre regime ... It has continued to request aid [from Congress] for Somalia even while admitting that the government it seeks to assist has murdered and driven out hundreds of thousands of its own citizens and destroyed their homes and cities."[27]

Barre was successfully ousted from power in 1991. But the political crisis and military conflict persisted as various groups fought for control over the state. To make matters worse drought and famine gripped the south of the country the following year. By the end of 1992, however, rain had come and the famine began to subside. At the same time, conflict between rival factions was also starting to settle. At this point President Bush decided that a military intervention in Somalia could provide a public relations boost for his country's armed forces, along with creating a precedent for similar adventures in the future. Colin Powell, then-Chairman of the Joint Chiefs of Staff, described it as a "paid political advertisement."[28] The U.S. used its sway to bring the United Nations along for the ride. Countries like Belgium and Canada, as well as the likes of Nigeria and Pakistan, sent troops. A U.S.-led UN Security Council-sanctioned task force arrived in Somalia in December 1992.

The PR stunt did not go as planned. The presence of foreign troops who were mandated by the Security Council to use "all necessary measures" to establish control greatly exacerbated the situation. The population quickly turned openly hostile against the UN mission as a result of the cruel treatment Somalis received from UN troops. The use of overwhelming firepower, with seemingly little regard for distinguishing between civilians and combatants, was a persistent feature of the "humanitarian intervention." As the researcher Alex de Waal notes, "Accounts of the fighting frequently contain such statements as this: 'One moment there was a crowd, and the next instant it was just a bleeding heap of dead and injured.'"[29]

Shameless even in the face of unceasing controversy, the UN proclaimed that the undertaking in Somalia was a success. The first phase was particularly celebrated, accompanied by boasts that up to two million victims of famine had been saved. The real figures would be estimated to be between 10,000 and 25,000. "Much more modest forms of relief aid," de Waal points out, "could have achieved exactly the same result,"[30] not to mention the destruction that could have been avoided, and a political situation that could have been held back from heading further towards disarray.

Going through several phases, and failing each time to establish stability, the intervention ended in March 1995 with all foreign troops pulling out of the country.[31] The Security Council declared that "the people of Somalia bear the ultimate responsibility for achieving national reconciliation and restoring peace to Somalia."[32] Suddenly abandoned by its erstwhile saviors Somalia continued to remain mired in conflict, with rival warlords carving out fiefdoms for themselves. Mirroring its fringe status as a country without a central government, Somalia for the time being was relegated to the margins of global diplomacy.

It would not remain there for long. As the War in Afghanistan was launched, the George W. Bush administration feared that members of al-Qaeda, deeming Somalia's lack of a government a positive feature, would relocate to the country.[33] It was decided that the counterterrorism strategy for Somalia needed to be overhauled. As part of this new strategy, the Central Intelligence Agency (CIA) began funding Somali warlords to carry out assassinations of suspected terrorists. Predictably, the aggrandized warlords were inclined to use their newly acquired resources to wreak havoc across the country.

In response to this new spike in chaos, the population rallied to support an umbrella group calling itself the Islamic Courts Union (ICU). Bringing together twelve disparate groups, the ICU saw itself as a pragmatic alliance that could establish some stability. It happened to be the case that a few elements in the ICU held a militant Islamist outlook. But these elements were marginal, hardly poised to have a controlling influence over the ICU. Thirsty for blood in its War on Terror, such subtlety was lost on Washington.

With the ICU gaining a steady foothold, the U.S.-backed warlords banded together to declare war against the group in early 2006. The Alliance for the Restoration of Peace and Counterterrorism (the group's name was likely devised by the CIA) would be routed in combat by the ICU in a matter of months. The fact that the Alliance was being funded and armed by Washington[34] did not help it in the end. Somalis had had enough of the murderous warlords. They volunteered in large numbers to join the fight against them. The ICU's victory was well worth it. The numerous roadblocks put up by the warlords were dismantled, resulting in a dramatic decline in food prices. A calm was achieved in Mogadishu that had not existed since before Barre's ouster.

During the war launched by the U.S.-backed warlords, al-Shabab definitively made itself known, allying itself with the ICU.[35] The journalist Jeremy Scahill notes that al-Shabab adopted the "warlords' own tactics against them, assassinating figures associated with the CIA's warlord alliance," and were quick to display a knack for ruthlessness.[36] Al-Shabab was not only a militant Islamist group, unlike other similarly-minded elements associated with the ICU, which were inward looking, it saw itself as part of the global jihadist movement and had secure ties with al-Qaeda.

Immediately after its triumph over the warlords, the ICU tried to dissociate itself from the likes of al-Shabab. Sheikh Sharif, the head of the ICU, wrote a letter to the U.S. embassy in Nairobi stating that his group stood against terrorism and would be willing to "invite an investigative team from the United Nations to make sure that international terrorists do not use the region as a transit route or hiding ground."[37] The overture was not welcome. Washington began planning the overthrow of the ICU. It was the backlash from the chaos and conflict spread by the U.S.-backed warlords that allowed al-Shabab to emerge from the shadows. And U.S. actions would help to ensure that al-Shabab's star kept rising.

It was determined that Ethiopia, Somalia's hated neighbor, would serve as a U.S. proxy for removing the ICU and installing a government that appeared more amenable to Washington.[38] In the lead up to the late 2006 Ethiopian invasion, a propaganda campaign was conducted against the ICU. For instance, Jendayi Frazer, the top Bush administration official on Africa, proclaimed: "The Council of Islamic Courts is now controlled by al-Qaeda cell individuals."[39] Such statements were categorically false. This seemed to matter little to the media, which, as Scahill documents, played its usual role as lapdog to the powerful:

> Much like the buildup to the 2003 Iraq invasion, major U.S. media outlets began hyping the al-Qaeda connection, printing the views of anonymous U.S. officials as verified facts. Sensational headlines began appearing, warning of a "Growing Al-Qaeda Menace in Africa." Corporate TV reporters breathlessly offered up revisionist history of the Somalia conflict, conveniently omitting the U.S. role in creating the crisis. On CBS, veteran correspondent David Martin declared, "Somalia has been a safe haven for Al-Qaeda ever since the U.S. military pulled out of the country following the infamous Black Hawk Down firefight." CNN's Pentagon correspondent Barbara Starr practically sounded like a Bush administration spokesperson: "Today, here in East Africa, the concern remains that unless Somalia is shut

down as a terrorist safe haven, the threat of another attack remains very real."[40]

ICU leaders were forced to go on the run as the Ethiopian army invaded Somalia. U.S. air power was employed to hunt the ICU leaders down. While this strategy worked to an extent for taking out people associated with the ICU, it was much more effective at killing and maiming civilians. The Ethiopian troops, too, were quite proficient at abusing the general population. Rape and wanton murder followed in their wake. It was this setting that allowed al-Shabab, which possessed an unrivaled ability to mete out and bear cruelty, to achieve prominence. As Scahill points out, "With the ICU dismantled and the brutal Ethiopian occupation continuing for nearly three more years, al-Shabab emerged as the vanguard in the fight against foreign occupation."

Pushed to the brink, Somalia was turned into a land where those who could manage to be more ruthless than the rest achieved control over the largest amount of area. Thus, when the famine struck, al-Shabab was in place to further victimize its victims. Such "leaders who create hardships for their own citizens" certainly deserve to be condemned. But those who have created the conditions that allowed these "leaders" to come to power are much more deserving of condemnation. An accurate account of history, however, was conveniently missing from media reports about the famine. What we heard instead, as we always hear, was a story in which the West was benevolent. The West, we are repeatedly told, is charitable.

BLEEDING MONEY

Most of those who live in the rich world seem to be thoroughly convinced, no doubt in large part due to the efforts of the media, that their countries represent a positive force around the planet. Consider, for instance, the results of a 2010 poll that asked U.S. citizens to estimate the amount of the federal budget that goes towards foreign aid. The median guess was that an enormous 25 percent of the annual budget was allotted for overseas assistance. The real figure is less than 1 percent.[41] If the trivial amounts of aid given by the likes of the U.S. are disappointing, the amount of wealth that leaves the poor world for the rich is absolutely shocking.

As of 1998 the developing world was spending $13 to service its debt for every dollar that it received in grants.[42] Much of the debt accumulated by poor countries is odious. The borrowed money did not benefit the people who are now being forced to pay it back. At times it was used by tyrannical governments to make war against opposition groups and the common people. A large amount of the money simply left the developing world soon after it was borrowed, finding its way into the private bank accounts of corrupt government officials and other well-connected individuals.

Léonce Ndikuma and James Boyce estimate that between 1970 and 2008 for every dollar that was received in foreign debt by countries in sub-Saharan Africa, about sixty cents left as capital flight in the same year.[43] Those providing the loans are not, or should not be, unaware of the problem, as the money frequently ends up in the same banks that lent it. The authors conclude that "sub-Saharan Africa is a net creditor to the rest of the world in the sense that its foreign assets exceed its foreign liabilities."[44] For the thirty-three countries they look at, the total stock of capital flight was $944 billion in 2008. In comparison, the external debts of these countries amounted to $177 billion in the same year. Rather than being a "bottomless pit," Africa seems to be a wellspring of riches from which only foreigners are benefitting.

"Africa is bleeding money," Ndikuma and Boyce write.[45] The violent imagery is appropriate. Considering that so much of the money that leaves the continent is meant for government development schemes, the large human cost of illegal capital flight should be obvious. Countless people across the continent needlessly die from easily treatable diseases. Millions go hungry and suffer from want of clean water. Children are stunted, their physical and mental capacities cut short. And instead of doing something to stop the outflow of money that could be put to much needed use, we dole out a meager amount of charity.

For us as a society to give aid to the poor while we continue to make things worse for them is akin to me helping to stitch someone's wounds with one hand while I repeatedly stab her with the other. The stitches I sew may be of help to her but the more important effect they have, as far as I figure things, will be to cover up the harm I have done and continue to do.

While Singer notes that we contribute to the misery of the poor, he fails to meaningfully explore the systemic dimensions of this matter. One of the examples he uses is climate change. Rich countries have released, and continue to release, disproportionate amounts of greenhouse gases. The harmful effects of these gases will disproportionately fall upon the developing world. Not only does the geographical location of poor countries make them especially vulnerable to climate change, but also their lack of resources prohibits them from defending against its impacts.

Singer makes the argument that since our greenhouse gas emissions are hurting poor countries we have a moral obligation to give them aid to offset the harm.[46] He does not point out that we first have a moral obligation to stop spewing greenhouse gases into the atmosphere. It could be said that he perhaps hints at this point when he chastises certain ultra-rich individuals who sail around in giant yachts that consume large amounts of fuel. One can infer that, to the extent Singer believes in stopping the harm we are doing—through greenhouse gas emissions and otherwise—his position is that we should do so by making less harmful lifestyle choices.

That is to say, we should consume smaller amounts of meat, purchase organic fruits and vegetables, and drive our cars less often to lower our carbon footprint. We should also perhaps purchase fair-trade goods to make a contribution to undoing the unfairness of traditional trade. In short, we should be "conscious consumers." As we saw in the previous chapter, this kind of individualistic, apolitical approach to activism has little chance of creating large-scale social change.

There is also the issue that charity creates distance. Just as it seeks to erase material inequality, it enhances inequality of a different sort. It raises the social regard and self-esteem of the donor, and lowers that of the receiver.

This is not good. It is not to a society's credit (global though it may be) to have one group of human beings indebted and subservient to another. While on its own terms this is troubling enough, it is doubly so given the existing relationship between wealth and poverty.

Because of their higher position in the transaction, those who give charity are prone to developing condescending perspectives. Singer himself falls victim to this. In one instance, he writes approvingly about a development organization that provides materials for schools, but makes sure that locals in the communities being helped contribute their labor to the task of construction. "The work the villagers put in gives them sweat equity," Singer tells us, "which makes them far more committed to seeing the school succeed."[47] Concepts like "sweat equity" are common within the so-called development community. Poor people should not be given handouts, the refrain goes;

they will not be able to truly understand the value something has unless they work for it. They would also, it is sometimes absurdly argued, become lazy as they would come to expect that gracious Westerners will look after their needs regardless of how hard they work. This, ironically, comes from people who rank as the top receivers of handouts in the world.

Residents of rich countries receive tremendous amounts of protection, goods, and services from their governments. These include public education, universal healthcare (except in the U.S.), minimum wage laws, food safety guidelines,. and clean drinking water. One does not ever hear the case being made that residents of rich countries do not value education because the vast majority of them have not been involved in the construction of schools. Yet, we are told that if a school was built in a poor village and the residents were not forced to put in "sweat equity," they would not be able to appreciate its value.

Though gracious Westerners may think otherwise, the poor are not stupid. Appreciation for the value of education has not passed them by. As one group of researchers documents in *Voices of the Poor*, the poor consistently express concern about their children's education, or lack of it.[48] And it is not only the words of the poor that reveal their concern for education; their actions do too.

Some governments use cash transfer programs to encourage poor families to send their children to school—transfers can be seen as a way to make up for the loss of school-going children's income. Cash transfers are often given on the condition that parents send their children to school. A study done by the World Bank to find the importance of conditionality in cash transfers discovered that there was *no difference* in school enrollment rates between groups who received transfers with conditionality, and those who received transfers without conditionality.[49] When it comes to sending their children to school, it would seem that impoverished households are not so much in need of goading, whether by means of conditionality or "sweat equity," as they are in need of financial support.

As for the matter of laziness, it takes a stretch of the imagination to believe the claim that, for instance, villagers who are accustomed to farming long hours in unkind weather using rude implements will all of a sudden become indolent if a healthcare center, school, or well is constructed for them. If residents of rich countries can avoid descending into perpetual lethargy despite all of the handouts they receive, the outcome for the poor will not be any different considering the much smaller amount of handouts they are bound to be given.

MARKET-BASED SOLUTIONS?

Increasingly, NGOs working in poor countries do not consider what they are involved in as charity. They insist, instead, that they are doing "development work"—or simply "development." All too often one finds that this is just a fancy way to refer to charity. There are, however, certain things that NGOs are involved in which truly cannot be described as charity. Included among these is the promotion of market-based solutions to poverty. But is it actually the case that such approaches contribute to development and poverty reduction?

Perhaps the most popular market-based approach to poverty reduction is microfinance. To many of those who endorse microfinance, the poor are intrepid "entrepreneurs" who, if only they had access to small amounts of credit, would be able to get themselves out of poverty. The term "entrepreneurship" has been adopted to refer to the work done by those who are self-employed in the informal sector of the economy in order to portray the poor as empowered individuals. The point is to counter their depiction as worthy only of our pity. While the gesture may be well-meant, as far as the truth is concerned depicting the poor as shabbily-dressed business people who are the masters of their own destinies is hardly an improvement over depicting them as only-to-be-pitied creatures.

The reality of working in the informal economy is quite a bit drearier than the romanticized image often put before us. Being an "entrepreneur" in a poor country tends to involve hawking petty merchandise in crowded areas, including at busy intersections where the heat and the choking exhaust fumes mix to create an oppressive work environment. In the end, the demanding effort put into dodging cars and pestering pedestrians generates miniscule amounts of income.

The poor hardly ever willfully engage in "entrepreneur-ship," if it can really be called that. They do it because they have no choice. Most of them would much rather have stable jobs than deal with the havoc of self-employment in the informal sector.[50] No doubt this is because they understand that, instead of being a way out of poverty, more often than not "entrepreneurship" will only guarantee them continued misery. What is more, making microloans available to the poor does not help very much.

Though NGOs keep relating the same tired jingoes about the supposed magic of microfinance, the evidence is hardly encouraging. In recent years, news stories about microlending agencies behaving like loan sharks have shaken some public confidence in microfinance. But we have been assured that such cases are deviations from the norm, and that in general microfinance should continue to be seen as an important tool in the fight against poverty. Even when things go smoothly, however, the results are disappointing. Anecdotes aside, the cumulative data make clear that microfinance *does not* help the poor escape poverty. As David Roodman and Jonathan Murdoch put it, "30 years into the microfinance movement we have little solid evidence that it improves the lives of clients in measurable ways."[51]

The high interest rates make it difficult for borrowers to profit enough from an investment to successfully repay loans. In some places, the aggressive lending practices of microfinance agencies has led to arrangements where people borrow from one place to pay off the loan from another, eventually resulting in a spate of late payments and defaults that have left the local microfinance industry facing collapse.[52] Even where things do not take such a dramatic turn, the best that microfinance seems to offer the poor is a way to smooth out their consumption by making up for shortcomings in the funds they have on hand—rather than being used to spur on business activity, the poor tend to end up relying on microloans for such things as paying rent and covering the doctor's bill.[53]

The shortcomings of microfinance are symptomatic of "private sector-led development" schemes in general. Throughout modern history poverty reduction and development have been successfully brought about not by the leadership of the private sector, but through state-led efforts. As the development economist Lance Taylor explains, "Import substitution [through state intervention] is about the only way anybody's ever figured out to industrialize ... The state has always intervened to create a capitalist class, and then it has to regulate the capitalist class, and then the state has to worry about being taken over by the capitalist class, but the state has always been there."[54]

The infatuation with the market so often on display among NGOs is the result of an uncritical acceptance of the creed promoted by the age of individualism. Whereas according to the supporting narrative of our age, the market represents freedom and choice, it is often in fact exactly the opposite. As we have already noted, for a

Bangladeshi sweatshop worker faced with destitution and ruin the "freedom of contract" is no freedom at all. Rather than being put in a position where they have to face the full force of opportunistic behavior characteristic of the marketplace, the poor need to be provided protection against it.

As an example of what the poor are up against, one can look at the markets for drinking water that have arisen in and around the urban slums of the Third World. In places like Nairobi and Mumbai, enterprising individuals who are rich enough to have the municipal government send tap water to their homes have discovered that they can sell this water forward at extortionate rates to slum dwellers. The poor, as a result, can end up being charged tens of times more than the rich for the same water.[55]

The poor need to be protected from the abuse their vulnerability makes them subject to by their employers. They need to be protected from unscrupulous merchants who sell harmful counterfeit medicines. Poor farmers need protection against the subsidized agricultural products from rich countries that undercut their prices. And so on. Ultimately, however, we need to recognize that a global market system that relies on the existence of massive amounts of inequality to function will never be able to provide sufficient amounts of protection and justice to the poor. Our concern for the fate of the impoverished should lead us to challenge this system outright, not merely try to make slight adjustments to it.

SOLIDARITY, NOT CHARITY

When it comes to truly addressing the problems of global poverty, charity, as we have seen, will not do. We cannot simply try to deal with poverty by trying to address its symptoms. We have to rid the world of the structures that produce it, and place in their stead structures that are more just. It makes little sense to, as Oscar Wilde puts it, "try to solve the problem of poverty ... by keeping the poor alive ... The proper aim is to try to reconstruct society on such a basis that poverty will be impossible."[56]

Despite the strong criticisms offered here against charity my point is not to suggest that we should refrain from giving to charity altogether. If a homeless man was to walk up to me on the street and ask me for money so he could buy breakfast it would not be an appropriate response for me to say, "Sorry, I can't give you money because I think charity is immoral and helps to keep in place the existing structures that produce poverty. Don't worry, though, I'm working with others to make sure these structures change in the long run." Of course, to satisfy immediate needs charity can be a useful tool. It should not, however, be seen as a substitute for efforts aiming to change the societal structures that are responsible for creating poverty to begin with.

The kinds of structures that are of particular interest to us are ones that facilitate the exploitation of the poor. And in assessing the problems of poverty and their connection to exploitation, an understanding of the ways in which we fit into the nexus of exploitation and injustice is of critical importance. A commonly held perception is that the flip-side of Third World exploitation is First World advantage. While this may be true on the surface, a deeper investigation reveals a more nuanced picture.

Cecil Rhodes, mining magnate and founder of Rhodesia (now Zimbabwe), advocated support for the British Empire based on the notion that resources from the colonies, particularly food, would help to quell working class resentment. In 1895, he wrote:

> I was in the East End of London yesterday and attend-ed a meeting of the unemployed. I listened to the wild speeches, which were just a cry for 'bread', 'bread!' and on my way home I pondered over the scene and I became more than ever convinced of the importance of imperialism ... The Empire, as I have always said, is a bread and butter question. If you want to avoid civil war, you must become imperialists.[57]

Rhodes was to a large extent being disingenuous. Rather than concern for the downtrodden, his advocacy on behalf of imperialism was likely rooted in the fact that the Empire was of tremendous benefit to capitalists like himself. While the costs of Empire fell upon the public, in the home country and especially in the colonies, private enterprises reaped stupendous rewards. But Rhodes was not wrong about the benefits of cheap commodities in restraining discontent among the masses. Imperialism continues to serve a similar purpose to this day, though the particulars differ.

It is important to note that significant portions of marginalized populations within rich countries—indigenous peoples, other minorities, migrant workers, the elderly, single mothers—live in dire conditions, which do not necessarily compare favorably to the Third World. Black men in Harlem, for example, are less likely to live beyond the age of forty than men in Bangladesh.[58] That said, there no longer exists a "cry for bread" among the majority of residents in imperialist countries. Material conditions have improved significantly since the nineteenth century.

Today, quite apart from quelling resentment over access to basic needs, the cheap commodities obtained through the exploitation of the Third World serve to feed the overconsumption of the masses in rich countries. But just as providing basic standards of living helped to suppress anger, the conspicuous consumption the masses are compelled to take part in serves to restrain the onset of their enlightenment. Concerns about MP3 players, cars, and shiny dresses stand in for more meaningful endeavors. Commitment to the community, the notion that education could be a means to achieve personal growth, and ideals concerning justice are warped and diminished. It turns out that consumerism, a product of modernity, and not antiquated religion is the opium of the masses. The moral depravity of our present arrangement, in which the poor are oppressed so that the rich can lead vacuous lives, brings to mind the bitter condemnation of racial inequality by the black author Richard Wright in his 1945 autobiography:

The essence of the irony of the plight of the Negro in America, to me, is that he is doomed to live in isolation while those who condemn him seek the basest goals of any people on the face of the earth. Perhaps it would be possible for the Negro to become reconciled to his plight if he could be made to believe that his sufferings were for some remote, high, sacrificial end; but sharing the culture that condemns him, and seeing that a lust for trash is what blinds the nation to his claims, is what sets storms to rolling in his soul.[59]

As exploitation and overconsumption are coupled, in order to put a stop to one, attention must be given simultaneously to the other. When we struggle for change in this light, it is not a matter of giving charity. We struggle, rather, in solidarity with the poor for the freedom of all of humanity.

CHAPTER 3

Climate Change and Activism

*If you think you can solve a serious environmental
question like global warming without actually
confronting the question of by whom and how the
foundational value structure of our society is being
determined, then you are kidding yourself.*

—David Harvey[1]

Human beings have altered the surroundings we have
resided in for as long as we have been on the planet.
Though not all of our alterations can be characterized as
exceedingly harmful to the biosphere and other species,
history is littered with many examples of alterations that
can be characterized as such. Even in prehistoric times,
long before we discovered metallurgy and gunpowder,
we managed to hunt several species of large mammals
to extinction. This happened as we made our way to new

continents like Australia and the Americas, where other forms of life had not evolved alongside us and, thus, were not attuned to our cleverness.[2] With permanent settlement and increasing numbers came localized forest clearances, diversion of rivers, draining of swamps, as well as air pollution. Traces of atmospheric lead pollution can be found in the polar ice caps onward from about 2000 years ago.[3] While many of the pre-industrial human effects on the environment were astonishing, they would be completely eclipsed in significance by what was to come.

For the past 250 years human behavior has influenced the planet to such a degree that the term *Anthropocene* has been coined to refer to the current geological epoch. The Holocene, which began about 12,000 years ago, is no more. A paper by members of the Stratigraphy Commission of the Geological Society of London explains: "The combination of extinctions, global species migrations, and the widespread replacement of natural vegetation with agricultural monocultures is producing a distinctive contemporary biostratigraphic signal. These effects are permanent, as future evolution will take place from surviving (and frequently anthropogenically relocated) stocks."[4] The earth's natural course of development has been forced to give way to the might of modern industrial civilization. Lest we fall into veneration of our own magnificence, however, we should take note that the trajectory we have brought into being is headed straight towards disaster. We are making the planet unliveable.

Large hydro dams, intensive agriculture, and construction practices are stripping away soils faster than they can be replenished by natural rates of sedimentation. Rivers, lakes, and groundwater aquifers are becoming polluted and drying up. One of the most dramatic examples of the latter is Lake Chad, which has shrunk to 10 percent of its original size. Deforestation continues at alarming rates. Desertification is rife. The Sahara, for instance, is expanding southward at a rate of almost fifty kilometers every year. Waters at the surface of the ocean are acidifying while the seabed is being devastated by fishing trawlers. The planet's health, described in terms of its ability to support life, is visibly in decline.

According to one estimate, populations of vertebrate species—mammals, reptiles, birds, amphibians, and many types of fish—have fallen on average by a staggering 28 percent from 1970 to 2008.[5] To add to these worrying trends, and related to many of them, average global temperature is fast increasing.

This chapter discusses the severity of the threat posed by human-made climate change, the status of global negotiations, what needs to be done to avert the threat, and why we have so far failed to take meaningful action. The main thesis mirrors the one delivered in the previous chapter: the climate crisis (like global poverty) is a product of the capitalist system.

BEFORE THE CATACLYSM

The coming of the Holocene brought about a stabilization of the global temperature and sea level. A moderately warm and stable climate allowed agriculture to mature and unchanging coastlines served as habitats for thriving fish populations close to land. These developments facilitated the creation of permanent human settlements, which, in turn, led to the coming about of complex forms of credit, record-keeping, writing, philosophy, and science. In other words, modern human society was enabled by the prolonged interval of stable climate that characterized the Holocene. And it is precisely the conditions that allowed us to achieve our present state that we set ourselves up to change by unrelentingly emitting greenhouse gases into the atmosphere.

Much of the energy the Earth absorbs from the sun is reemitted away from the planet as infrared radiation. Naturally existing greenhouse gases, such as water vapor and carbon dioxide, stop a portion of the infrared radiation from leaving the atmosphere. This is the *natural* greenhouse effect. Without it life on the planet would not be possible. By emitting gases like carbon dioxide, methane, nitrous oxide, and chlorofluorocarbons (CFCs) into the atmosphere, human beings are contributing to the *enhancement* of the greenhouse effect. Smaller amounts of infrared radiation are able to leave the atmosphere as a result, leading to global warming.

This is not the first time that the earth's climate is changing. Throughout its history, the planet has seen large variations in temperature. At different times, various natural processes have been responsible for climate change. One cause has been the teetering of earth's axis.[6] Gravity from other planets, mainly Jupiter and Saturn, results in the axis around which the earth rotates swaying back and forth slightly. Over the course of 41,000 years the earth goes from a maximum tilt of 24.5° to a minimum tilt of 22.1° and then back again. If the earth is at its maximum tilt and starts to straighten, the poles will progressively receive less sunlight, allowing larger amounts of ice to form on them. A less pronounced tilt towards the sun also means that summers will be colder, resulting in less snowmelt. More ice means that larger amounts of sunlight will be reflected away from the earth. Thus, a straightening tilt can start to make the planet gradually cooler.

As temperatures decrease, the solubility of carbon dioxide in water increases. This means that as the planet becomes cooler and ocean temperature falls, more atmospheric CO_2 is taken in by the oceans. Since carbon dioxide is a greenhouse gas, smaller amounts of it in the atmosphere results in greater amounts of infrared radiation leaving the atmosphere, which causes further cooling. Additional decreases in temperature lead to more ice and more reflected sunlight, which in turn results in even more cooling, which again lowers the concentration of carbon dioxide in the atmosphere and so on. As this process carries on over thousands of years, the planet may experience large amounts of global cooling.[7]

The crucial difference between most instances of naturally occurring climate change and human-made climate change is the time scale. The natural processes that led the average global temperature to change took millennia to unfold. This meant that life on the planet had time to adapt to the changes. Adaptation could come about through biological changes as well as by physically moving to more habitable locations. Despite this, life could still find itself put under large amounts of strain and species could become extinct. In comparison to most natural processes that can cause climate change, human-made global warming is progressing at alarming rates. Since 1880 average surface temperature has risen by 0.8°C. The majority of this rise in temperature, about 0.5°C, has taken place since 1980. While this may seem like a small increase in temperature, it is of vast significance to the global climate system.

Temperature increases register unevenly across the planet, and the poles are the most sensitive to warming — since 1950 the air above the West Antarctic peninsula has warmed by almost 6°C.[8] Sea levels have started to rise because of melting polar ice caps. Mountaintop glaciers around the world are in retreat, endangering the fresh water supplies of hundreds of millions of people. Tropical storms, heat waves, and increased precipitation are all becoming more common. While the changes brought about by the rise in average global temperature may have gone largely unfelt by residents of rich countries, the situation is quite different for the poor of the world.

Those who have had little to do with causing the warming are suffering greatly as a result of it. A rise in the frequency of extreme weather events, expanded ranges of vector-borne diseases like malaria, and growing vulnerability of food production and water supplies is adding to the hardship the impoverished have to deal with. Tulsi Khara, a 70-year-old woman who lives in West Bengal, a delta region especially vulnerable to climate change, related the following:

> We are not educated people, but I can sense some-
> thing grave is happening around us. I couldn't be-
> lieve my eyes—the land that I had tilled for years,
> that fed me and my family for generations, has
> vanished. We have lost our livelihood. All our be-
> longings and cattle were swept away by cyclones ...
> It wasn't like this when I was young. Storms have
> become more intense than ever. Displacement and
> death are everywhere here. The land is shrinking
> and salty water gets into our fields, making them
> useless. We feel very insecure now.[9]

It is estimated that every year 400,000 people in poor countries die, while hundreds of millions are seriously affected, as a result of the global warming that has created so far.[10] It deserves to be noted that this is a close moral equivalent of a coalition of rich countries systematically rounding up and executing 400,000 people from the Third World every year, to say nothing about all those who are displaced, fall ill, go hungry or face other adversities as a result climate change. And, of course, as more warming sets in these numbers will only rise.

As there is a lag in time between the initial release of greenhouse gases and the warming they cause, we have yet to feel the full effect of the gases that have been released into the atmosphere. It is estimated that a total of 1.4°C in warming above the pre-industrial average will occur as a result of the greenhouse gases emissions to date.[11] According to the Intergovernmental Panel on Climate Change (IPCC) we need to stay below 2°C if we are to avoid especially adverse effects, and even this target has drawn significant criticism from prominent climate scientists for being too modest.[12] In any case, the 1.4°C in warming we have already set into motion will itself cause great amounts of destruction, and there are no signs that action is being taken to reach even the modest goals set by the IPCC.

Keeping global temperatures from rising above 2°C will require an 80 percent reduction in global greenhouse gas emissions by 2050.[13] Yes, *80 percent*! This radical reduction in emissions over such a short period of time would invariably involve making changes to the fossil fuel dependent lives that the populations of rich countries lead. We would readily notice sweeping changes being made to our surroundings and the way we live. Except for the availability of efficient light bulbs, talk about "green cars," and empty promises from politicians, there do not seem to be very many changes occurring around us. Life goes on as usual. And instead of decreasing, global greenhouse gas emissions continue to increase.

If this trend is not reversed, we will trigger amplifying climate feedbacks, such as releasing the massive natural reserves of methane locked in arctic permafrost, and activate runaway climate change. Simply put, this will lead to cataclysmic outcomes.

The few instances in history that parallel our current trajectory do not provide us with encouraging insight. About 251 million years ago the earth witnessed the kind of rapid climate change we are set on bringing about. The result was mass-extinction—some 90 percent of all species on the planet were exterminated. Sometimes referred to as the Great Dying, an incident such as this one could very well be recreated thanks to human-made global warming.

There will be much to worry about, however, even before the cataclysm. As the title of NASA scientist James Hansen's book *Storms of My Grandchildren* suggests, the transition from here to utter catastrophe will be, quite literally, a stormy one. Increasingly warmer global temperatures mean that the concentration of water vapor in the atmosphere is rising, which provides more energy to storms—cyclones, hurricanes, thunderstorms, and the like. Also, as a consequence of warming ocean temperatures, the range in which harsh tropical storms develop is becoming larger.[14] Hurricane Sandy, which led to dozens of deaths and tens of billions of dollars in damage when it hit the eastern United States in October 2012, is a sign of things to come in the next several decades.[15]

As a result of the combination of harsher storms and a rise in sea levels, coastal cities and low-lying nations around the world will be devastated. Increased rates of drought, floods, and fires will make food shortages commonplace. The resulting refugee crises will without doubt lead to disorder and conflict, as such events often do today. As the scale of these crises continuously expands, we can expect social breakdown to eventually emerge. The ensuing chaos will leave no one untouched in our deeply interconnected world.

For now, and for the immediate future, climate change largely looks to be just another issue of inequality and injustice—the poor are suffering as a result of actions taken by the rich. As one would expect in such a case, the rich and powerful are not interested in meaningfully offsetting the harm climate change afflicts on the poor. They are looking to seemingly tried and tested solutions instead. As climate change increasingly batters the impoverished and they demand reprieve and amends, the rich will raise military spending and build secure livelihoods within barricaded compounds; they will recycle and compost all that they can, buy locally grown apples, and drive "green cars."

And, of course, there will routinely be occasions for them to dole out some charity.

Razor-wire fences and giant walls in the West Bank and along the U.S.-Mexico border may provide a sense of security to Israelis and Americans while they distract themselves inside their fortresses of consumption from the pain and suffering in which they are complicit. But the destruction caused by climate change will not long remain consigned to the poor. If nothing is done to halt the warming, the barricades will cease to be of use. Mitigation strategies and emergency response systems, too, will lose their effectiveness. The chickens, as they say, will have come home to roost. Yet, if their actions are any guide, the rich do not seem to be aware of this. There is no sign that they will make any meaningful efforts to prevent climate change from eventually jeopardizing their own way of life.

NEGOTIATING THE EARTH AWAY

The outcomes of global negotiations on climate change, which began at the 1992 Earth Summit in Rio de Janeiro, have been appalling. In Rio the nations of the world came together and agreed to stabilize "greenhouse gas concentrations in the atmosphere at a level that would prevent dangerous anthropogenic interference with the climate system. Such a level should be achieved within a time frame sufficient to allow ecosystems to adapt naturally to climate change, to ensure that food production is not threatened and to enable economic development to proceed in a sustainable manner."[16] The agreement was not much more than nice words. It did not establish binding requirements or lay out concrete steps to accomplish the objective. These, it was reasoned, could come later.

Finally, in 1997 a binding treaty was decided upon in Kyoto. Developed countries agreed to collectively cut their annual greenhouse gas emissions by an average of about 5 percent for the period of 2008–2012 relative to their emissions in 1990. Kyoto was proclaimed a triumph of global cooperation—a united stand against a common challenge.

It was, in fact, a sham and a failure. A large amount of hubbub has been made about the U.S. not ratifying the accord and Canada, after having ratified it, withdrawing from it. These, however, were not the reasons for Kyoto's failure. It was useless from the beginning.

The treaty's uselessness is easily demonstrated by the fact that it allowed rich countries to "offset" their emissions by funding tree planting and other emissions reduction projects in poor countries. Even if offset schemes were implemented properly (as it will shortly become clear, this was not at all the case) they would do nothing to reduce overall emissions—any reductions made in the developing world imply that an equal amount of emissions are released in rich countries. "Buying and selling carbon offsets," writes the environmental journalist George Monbiot, "is like pushing the food around on your plate to create the impression that you have eaten it."[17]

We also need to consider the fact that planting trees that will take in carbon dioxide over several decades does very little to offset the harmful effects of greenhouse gases being emitted into the atmosphere *today*.[18] The fact that Kyoto regards tree planting as an adequate substitute for emissions reductions is in itself a clear indication that the treaty was a joke.

But it gets worse. There has been little monitoring over the process of accounting for offsets, resulting in a large amount of fraud. Upon investigation, offset projects have often been found to be overhyped. In other cases, they have turned out to have been altogether nonexistent.[19] (In such instances the environment may not have been better off as a result of the offset projects, but the private companies and NGOs given money to implement them certainly benefitted.)

Perhaps the most brazen abuses of the offsetting regime have involved creative entrepreneurs who learned to game the system. Factories in China, India, Mexico, and elsewhere have been earning carbon credits worth tens of millions of dollars simply by producing a highly polluting coolant gas and then destroying it. The gas in question is HFC-23, a greenhouse gas 11,700 times more potent than carbon dioxide. Between the years 2005 and 2012 more than 40 percent of the carbon credits granted under the UN's offset scheme were given to coolant factories.[20]

Despite Kyoto— or more correctly, because of it—global greenhouse gas emissions were 40 percent higher in 2008 than in 1990. Emissions in developing countries like China, India, and Brazil grew rapidly. Most of the developed countries that had agreed to emissions reductions failed to make the cuts. It was a matter of chance that some were successful in cutting emissions. Russia, for example, was able to achieve large cuts because after the dissolution of the Soviet Union it went through a phase of rapid deindustrialization.

As bad as Kyoto was, negotiations since then have been a further step backwards. As Kyoto comes to an end, rich countries have declined so far to sign onto another binding treaty. According to them, voluntary accords will suffice for now. Big polluters from the developing world like China, India, and South Africa have also been given seats at the behind-the-scenes negotiating table. Won over by the prize of a mutually-assured "right to pollute," these countries have reneged on their previously held compacts with the rest of the Third World.[21] NGOs, too, have dutifully taken up their assigned position as helpers of the powerful. In advance of the 2010 climate negotiations in Copenhagen the celebrated anti-apartheid activist and poet Dennis Brutus offered the following reflection: "My own view is that a corrupt deal is being concocted in Copenhagen with the active collaboration of NGOs who have been bought off by the corporations, especially oil and transport. They may even be well-intentioned but they are barking up the wrong tree."[22]

To try to divert the justifiable anger of poor countries that are most vulnerable to global warming, the rich have made promises of trifling amounts of aid in the form of the Green Climate Fund. The Fund has not come into being because rich countries feel they owe a debt to the poor. Though they may have been responsible for creating climate change, we are told that this is apparently not the time to be assigning blame. As U.S. Special Envoy for Climate Change Todd Stern remarked, "The sense of guilt or culpability or reparations—I just categorically reject that."[23] Well, in that case the Fund must be the outcome of the goodwill the rich hold towards the poor, right? It actually is, of course, just a bit of hush-money — "we will continue to pollute while you shut your mouth and die"-money.

The charity will in no way make up for the damage global warming is going to cause in the Third World. By one estimate, the annual "climate debt" owed to poor countries by the rich will be $400 billion by 2020.[24] Rich countries are not willing to offer anywhere near this amount of money as part of the Green Climate Fund. As Patrick Bond points out, "Pakistan suffered $50 billion in climate-related flood damage alone in 2010, yet the total on offer from the North to the whole world was just $30 billion for 2010–2012." He explains that even this was "funny money" as some countries "were trying to pay their share partly in the form of loan guarantees, not grants."[25] This kind of chicanery is a mainstay of plans to address climate change. One thing is said and quite another thing is meant. The point is to make sure we do not in fact start doing what needs to be done.

WHAT NEEDS TO BE DONE

An effective strategy to rapidly cut the use of fossil fuels and defuse the climate crisis requires deliberate measures to be taken instead of vague commitments to voluntary action. Minimally, a straightforward and steadily increasing carbon tax is required to increase the cost of fossil fuels so that their use goes into decline. Instead of a direct tax on carbon, however, we are offered "cap-and-trade" schemes, which seek to create financial products out of the right to pollute. Cap-and-trade schemes are put forward because their workings are murky, allowing them to be easily implemented in ways that produce no results.

Along with putting in place restrictive carbon taxes, proactive schemes need to be devised and implemented to make the required deep cuts in emissions. We need to, for instance, actively redesign urban environments and retire the car as a primary form of transportation. All forms of transportation—of which private auto use is the largest constituent—make up 13 percent of global greenhouse gas emissions.[26] This number only accounts for emissions produced directly by vehicles, and does not include emissions resulting from vehicle manufacturing, extraction of fossil fuels used for transportation, and land-use changes related to transportation.

Car manufacturing—including mineral extraction, iron and steel production, as well as the car assembly itself—is perhaps the largest and most energy-intensive industrial scheme on the planet. Extracting and refining oil, carried out in large part in order to fuel cars, accounts for more than 6 percent of global emissions.[27] And each year, about one million acres of land are paved for roads, highways, and parking lots,[28] while urban sprawl facilitated by the car eats up even larger amounts of agricultural or undeveloped land.

While the health of the planet requires us to abandon the car, our social system is not hearing any of it. Car sales are a major indicator of the health of the economy and we are told that they must continuously grow. Seven months into 2012, as life on the planet was gasping for breath, governments and investors were sighing with relief when it was reported that, compared to the same time period in the previous year, car sales around the world were up 6 percent, with North America experiencing a rise of 12 percent.[29] All major economies except for the few struggling with the European sovereign debt crisis registered growth in car sales numbers. Following the global slump and recession of recent years, the economy was looking more securely back on track.

In place of retiring the private automobile altogether, car manufacturers have set about singing to us the ballad of the "green car." Between cars that run on bio-fuels, electric batteries, and hydrogen fuel cells, we are told that the future holds plenty of bright possibilities, so we do not have to fathom the seemingly lousy option of giving up our car-centric lifestyles. All of this is nothing but hype. New technologies are not going to make the car an environmentally-friendly piece of machinery. As Bianca Mugyenyi and Yves Engler make clear, "There is no such thing as a green car. The basic point is this: A model of transportation that relies on individuals hopping into two, four or eight thousand pound metal boxes to get from one place to another is utterly unsustainable."[30]

As pointed out in the first chapter, phasing out the use of cars and building walkable communities with secure access to public transit will have numerous positive effects in addition to lowering greenhouse gas emissions. It will mean, to name only a few things, less air pollution, more active lifestyles, and less onerous commutes to and from work. The processes, machinery, and skills currently being used to manufacture cars can be oriented towards developing actual green technologies. Just as bicycle paths and high-density neighborhoods come to replace roads and suburban sprawl in the living environment, the manufacture of buses, rail transit, as well as the likes of solar panels and wind turbines can replace cars in the industrial environment.

Cars and urban planning are, of course, only a piece of a larger puzzle. Along with lowering the consumption of cars, consumption in general must be central to this discussion. In 2008 depletion of resources such as fisheries and timber and disposal of carbon dioxide into the atmosphere was taking place at a rate that would require one and a half earths to sustain indefinitely.[31] If currently projected rates of growth of consumption and carbon emissions hold, by 2050 our "ecological footprint" will double. This projected trend has to go in the opposite direction. Of course, people who live in rich countries consume resources and produce waste at rates that are *far* higher than those who live in the Third World. If everyone on the planet lived the way Americans do, we would need four Earths. Thus, drastic cuts in consumption and waste production need to be made in rich countries.

Farming practices have to be reformed to become less reliant on inorganic fertilizers and pesticides. These are produced by means of fossil fuels and upon use they release nitrous oxide, a greenhouse gas 300 times more potent than carbon dioxide. Cattle rearing must be brought down in scale and transformed in quality. This sector, when related land-use changes and other factors are taken into consideration, accounts for an incredible 18 percent of global greenhouse gas emissions.[32]

The amount of energy consumed and wasted by buildings must be reduced through retrofitting and improved design. Currently, buildings account for 65 percent of electricity consumption and 30 percent of greenhouse gas emissions in the U.S.[33] Electrical grids have to be upgraded so that transmission losses are cut down and intermittent sources of energy like solar and wind can be better utilized. Electricity production through the use of fossil fuels needs to be rapidly phased out and replaced with renewable sources. Hansen takes the position that worldwide coal emissions must be ended completely by 2030 if we are to avert disaster.[34]

CLIMATE CHANGE GOES TO WAR

We are faced with a monumental task, to say the least. From a strictly technical standpoint, however, it is not especially daunting. The Second World War provides us with insight enough to know that the prompt realignment of societal objectives and people's livelihoods, as well as hurried technological advancement are possible. The massive scale on which the war was fought, not only in terms of the number of belligerents involved but also in the amount of resources mobilized, required a global makeover. A rapid reorientation on a global scale is certainly again possible. The knowledge, resources, and technological means available to us today should in theory make an easier job of such a project. Though looking back at the Second World War can tell us much, there exist crucial differences between the war and our present situation that will require us to take a comprehensively different route in achieving a new global transformation. In charting out our divergent course, it will be helpful to spot the differences.

First of all, the transformation we are looking to achieve today is quite a bit more profound that the kind brought into being by the war. During the war the focus of the existing economic arrangement was shifted towards the needs of the war (shipbuilding, munitions manufacturing, etc.) and then pushed into overdrive. While many consumer goods, even necessities, were in short supply, overall economic output expanded significantly. In our case overall economic output needs to *decline* as consumption is brought down to sustainable levels. As declining output is simply unthinkable within our present economic arrangement, the arrangement itself will have to be changed and not simply have its focus shifted.

Secondly, the war was a competitive undertaking, while our project is securely collaborative. There may have been large amounts of cooperation among those who were allied with each other, but the central objective of the war was to outcompete and destroy the opposing side. The task of building a sustainable world, on the other hand, requires cooperative engagement on an unprecedented scale. Competition, rivalry, and conflict have no place in the undertaking. If a collaborative spirit is not adopted and the usual politics of cynicism continue to rule the day, solutions to the problems we face will not be forthcoming. Negotiations on emissions reductions will remain petty games in which countries try to manoeuvre their way into agreements that let them get away with polluting as much as possible.

Depending upon the specific matter being considered, planning and action are variously required on local, regional, national, and global fronts. Wartime research needs to be and, because of its relatively narrow focus, can be secretive. By contrast, the diverse range and complex nature of the solutions we need demands that resources be collaboratively invested in various research areas to quickly improve design techniques and technologies. Moreover, transfer of appropriate green technologies has to be effected from rich countries to the poor so that the road to industrialization for developing countries is not an environmentally destructive one.

And a collective sense of responsibility needs to be adopted to deal with the hardships that will be encountered while we set about trying to remake the world. If we are to scale down livestock rearing, for instance, the 1.3 billion people around the world who rely on it for their livelihoods will surely find themselves put under stress as a result.[35] Since many of these people are poor and already have unstable livelihoods, forcing them to deal with increased adversity would hardly be just. As such, the road to take in scaling down would not be for rich countries to simply cut down the amount of beef they consume by putting import restrictions in place. Rather, along with putting measures in place that reduce beef consumption, countries should work together to create policies and invest resources into ensuring that secure livelihoods are found by those who have to abandon cattle rearing. If this kind of approach is not taken, tit-for-tat rivalries will negate the prospect of progress.

Third, and perhaps most importantly, the war was a tremendous boon for private capital, while the quest to achieve sustainability will invariably be against its interests. Thus, whereas capital had no reason to align itself against the war, it has every reason to try and impede our project. There are, of course, lots of tales being told today about how business is not only interested in working to build a more sustainable world, but that it will be intrepid investors and entrepreneurs in the marketplace who lead us to the green tomorrow.

This is complete nonsense. The private sector is not going to lead the advancement in technology required. Far from it. There is no way to reconcile the need to achieve sustainability with the overall interests of concentrated economic power. Actively working to reduce and level off economic output is not going to help anyone's profits.

In general, profit-seeking in the marketplace is simply not the engine of innovation we often think it to be. Private firms are certainly well-positioned to conduct research into and generate innovative ideas about matters that are readily marketable. However, the kind of research that has expensively long gestation periods and has diffuse, if any, commercial value, cannot be left to the private sector. As the economist Vernon Ruttan points out, the development of ground-breaking technologies like jet aviation, computers, nuclear power, satellites, semiconductors, and the internet was in large part the result of taxpayer funding—in these cases, through the U.S. military's research support and procurement.[36]

Green technologies like solar panels and wind turbines have a long way to go before they become cost-competitive in relation to traditional fossil fuel sources. Therefore, entrepreneurs and private investors cannot be expected to take the lead in bringing about the required technological development. Of course, the matter of priorities must also be considered. One would not expect the research conducted by General Motors, or any other auto manufacturer, to conclude that cars are a terrible way to travel. GM and its rival carmakers do, after all, have a product to sell. Hence, the biggest players in the transportation industry are dead set against creating a sustainable transportation system. (As we saw in the first chapter, the auto industry uses its economic and political sway to make sure the transportation system remains to its liking.)

The biggest players in the energy industry would likewise not be expected to resolve that fossil fuel use should be rapidly scaled down and the massive profits offered by it be voluntarily forfeited. Instead, their research gives us increasingly cleaner ways to extract fossil fuels, just as the car manufacturers have of late been giving us "green cars." At its oil sands operations in Alberta, for instance, Shell is happy to tell us that it employs a process called "hydrogen-addition," which allows it to produce a larger quantity of oil using the same amount of energy as older methods of oil production.[37] Of course, since the amount of oil Shell is producing in Alberta is always increasing, the efficiency gains do nothing to bring down the absolute amount of energy used.

In any case, the focus on technological solutions to the climate crisis is radically misplaced. According to inventor Saul Griffith, keeping the global average temperature below 2°C using simply technological means "would require building the equivalent of all the following:"

> a hundred square metres of new solar cells, fifty square metres of new solar-thermal reflectors, and one Olympic swimming pool's volume of genetically engineered algae (for biofuels) every second for the next twenty-five years; one three-hundred-foot-diameter wind turbine every five minutes; one hundred-megawatt geothermal-powered steam turbine

every eight hours; and one three-gigawatt nuclear
power plant every week.[38]

While technological advancements will no doubt be of help
in addressing the crisis, climate change is fundamentally
a social problem and it requires a social solution. The root
of the problem is a system that requires ever-growing
amounts of economic output to be sustained. A steady-
state capitalist economy is an utter impossibility. And
what we need before the establishment of a steady-
state economy is to shrink the size of the economy. For
capitalism, however, there is only one way to go—up.
David Harvey explains that our economic system is
driven by "capital," which is "not a thing but a process
in which money is perpetually sent in search of more
money."[39] One important outcome of this process is ever-
expanding economic output. As Harvey notes:

> Capitalists are always producing surpluses in the
> form of profit. They are then forced by competition
> to recapitalise and reinvest a part of that surplus
> in expansion. This requires that new profitable
> outlets be found ... The current consensus among
> economists and within the financial press is that a
> 'healthy' capitalist economy, in which most capital-
> ists make a reasonable profit, expands at 3 per cent
> per annum. Grow less than that and the economy
> is deemed sluggish. Get below 1 per cent and the
> language of recession and crisis erupts (many capi-
> talists make no profit).[40]

Instead of focusing on the inherent antagonism between the needs of capitalism and the well-being of the environment, we are continually being told tales about how maverick businesspeople will save the day. And while the oil and gas industry busies itself in boasting about the energy-saving innovations it has come up with, it is working incessantly—just like the auto industry and others—to shape the political landscape in its favor.

In 2011 the oil industry deployed 622 Washington lobbyists,[41] about three-fourths of whom had previously held employment with the federal government. This is, as the *Washington Post* explains, "a proportion that far exceeds the usual revolving door standards on Capitol Hill."[42] Former members of Congress accounted for eighteen of the lobbyists, while two were former directors of the Minerals Management Service (MMS), the agency tasked with regulating the industry.[43] Dozens more had previously been presidential appointees, aides of members of Congress, and employees of the MMS. On top of all this, the industry spends endless millions on lobbying and campaign contributions to elected officials.[44]

It makes perfect sense why everyone in Washington wants to make nice with the industry. Barack Obama, who certainly knows what it is like to be on the receiving end of the industry's generosity, brags: "I've directed my administration to open up millions of acres for gas and oil exploration across twenty-three different states. We're opening up more than 75 percent of our potential oil resources offshore. We've quadrupled the number of operating rigs to a record high. We've added enough new oil and gas pipeline to encircle the Earth and then some."[45]

For their part, legislators in Washington have repeatedly acted to stall progress in dealing with the climate crisis. Forget about taking meaningful measures such as actively phasing out the use of cars, even the most modest of measures evoke embittered scorn from policy-makers and are dutifully fought back. For instance, a 2012 bill that would have discontinued $2.5 billion in annual tax breaks received by the oil and gas sector—part of the $7 billion[46] in total annual tax breaks the sector receives—was voted down by the U.S. Senate.

This corporate *coup d'état* has been won not only through the direct cooption of elected officials, but also through a propaganda effort aimed at citizens. To build public support for keeping the $2.5 billion subsidy, the American Petroleum Institute (API) spent millions of dollars on an ad campaign that referred to the bill targeting the tax breaks as "another bad idea from Washington—higher taxes that could lead to higher prices."[47] The API maintains that it ran the campaign to "educate voters."[48] It turns out that the lesson was a shoddy one. The "new taxes" mentioned in the ads would not have been new at all. Rather, the bill would have forced companies to start paying *existing* taxes from which they are currently exempt. Also, while it is true, as mentioned in API's ads, that the passing of the bill "could actually raise gas prices," according to the Congressional Research Service the price increase would likely only have been one or two cents per gallon.[49] Having armed citizens with misinformation, the ads urged them to pressure their congressional representatives to vote to keep the tax breaks in place.

Aside from ad campaigns that help to drum up support for specific objectives held by the oil and gas industry, the public is bombarded with propaganda on behalf of the industry through the news media. The media are prone to giving undue consideration to the idea that natural variations in the climate can explain the warming that is currently taking place. The human origins of climate change are often presented alongside the "natural variations" perspective, relaying the false image that the latter explanation may be scientifically valid.

Pointing out the overwhelming agreement among scientists about the human origins of climate change, D. James Baker, a former administrator of the National Oceanic and Atmospheric Administration, stated the following in 1997: "There's a better scientific consensus on this than on any issue I know—except maybe Newton's second law of dynamics."[50]

The media, however, seem to have missed the memo. A study conducted by Maxwell and Joyce Boycoff randomly sampled newspaper articles covering global warming in the mainstream press from 1988 to 2002 and found that 53 percent of the articles gave approximately equal attention to the human origins of climate change and the "natural variations" perspective. 35 percent of the articles emphasized the perspective that climate change was occurring as a result of human activity but also gave some attention to the opposing view. Articles that presented the "natural variations" theory as the only valid way to explain climate change accounted for slightly higher than 6 percent of the sample. Finally, only slightly less than 6 percent of the articles focused strictly on the idea that the ongoing warming of the earth is a human-made phenomenon.[51]

As part of their study, the authors also looked at what the media have been saying about the actions that need be taken to avert the threat posed by global warming. They point out that "the scientific community has reached general consensus that immediate and mandatory actions are necessary to combat global warming."[52] The news media, however, persistently give undue support to the idea that we must be cautious, rather than urgent, in taking action to combat climate change. In the Boykoffs' study, articles that gave approximately equal attention to mandatory and voluntary measures, or urgent and cautious approaches, accounted for 78 percent of the sample. Those that favoured cautious and voluntary approaches made up slightly more than 11 percent of the sample, while slightly less than 11 percent of articles emphasized the need to take urgent and mandatory action.[53]

The Boykoffs posit that the news media's biased coverage is in large part the result of an insistence on trying to present a balanced picture. They argue that the attempt at balance is misplaced because the unscientific opinions of climate skeptics are not as deserving of attention as the scientifically verified reality of climate change. Thus, they contend that the media should refrain from trying to present a balanced picture where the science is so thoroughly in support of one side.[54] Unfortunately, this kind of moralizing can hardly be expected to work because the misinformation spread by the media about climate change, or other matters, has much more to do with structural factors than an insistence on balance. The concentration of ownership, source of funding, as well as the other "filters" discussed in the first chapter, make the news media a propaganda tool for political and economic power.

The media's painting of the climate crisis in ambivalent colors—the unwarranted attention given to "uncertainties"—has kept large portions of the public ignorant about the dangers of the threat we face. A 2010 Gallup poll found that 46 percent of Americans believe climate change is largely the result of "natural changes in the environment that are not due to human activities." In the same year 48 percent of Americans said that what they see in the news about the threat of global warming is "generally exaggerated"—this makes sense, as the same news stories that relate the dangers of climate change most often also work to quell worries about it.

Strikingly enough, as time has gone by and climate scientists have only become more certain about the human origins of climate change and more worried about the dangers it presents us with, American public opinion has gone in the opposite direction. In 1997 when Gallup first asked Americans what they thought about the presentation of climate change in the news media only

31 percent replied that it was "generally exaggerated." Likewise, in 2003 when Gallup began asking about the causes of climate change, only 33 percent answered that it was the result of "natural changes in the environment."[55] This trend in the wrong direction is, to say the least, most disturbing. With an increasingly confused public, the capitulation of the state and society to corporate interests remains ever more secure.

SELLING THE EARTH TO SAVE IT

"Confused" also happens to be an appropriate word to describe a large amount of the activism facing off against the climate crisis. Much of the attention of activists concerned about the environment, of course, revolves around individual lifestyle choices: following a "green" career path, eating locally produced food, conserving water, growing one's own food, recycling and composting as much as possible, etc. The object becomes to convince others to adopt similar lifestyles with ceaseless moralizing. It is not uncommon for activists to pronounce that the actions of individuals are the root of the problem. If everyone stopped "demanding" so many things, they tell us, corporations would not need to produce them. Such entreaties ignore the fact that for individuals *en masse* to adopt lifestyles that are not based around overconsumption would require them to be part of a completely different social context.

What about the kind of activism that moves beyond the individual and local and focuses on the global? Here too we find disappointment. The scene is dominated by large environmental NGOs—chief among them is the World Wide Fund for Nature (WWF), previously known as the World Wildlife Fund—who have been given a seat at the table at events where agreements on climate change are fashioned. These NGOs are apparently representatives of "civil society." Rather than staying in tune with those they advocate on behalf of, however, they seem more interested in retaining the favorable position they have been accorded by the powerful. Thus, while voicing limited amounts of dissent, they tend to go along with the market-based schemes devised by those who want to keep things from changing.

Among such schemes is one known as Reduced Emissions from Deforestation and Forest Degradation (REDD). This proposed strategy would seek to decrease emissions resulting from logging and forest encroachment in poor countries. Since deforestation is the source of almost one-fifth of global greenhouse gas emissions, this is an important area of focus. Unfortunately, there is little to suggest that the scheme will be effective. Its basis will be to attach a price to the carbon stored in forests. A developing country that reduces emissions related to deforestation will earn carbon credits. These credits could then be sold on international carbon markets where firms and rich governments looking to "offset" their emissions would purchase them.[56] An alternate funding arrangement would involve having an international fund created by rich governments to compensate poor countries for reducing deforestation-related emissions.

It is not difficult to predict that the widespread implementation of REDD will be accompanied by numerous problems. Just as the Clean Development Mechanism has been exploited by unscrupulous actors, REDD too will without doubt fall victim to fraud. Peter Younger, an environmental crimes specialist at Interpol, warns, "It is simply too big to monitor. The potential for criminality is vast and has not been taken into account by the people who set it up."[57] Younger warns that the lack of oversight will help to ensure that organized crime syndicates in Europe will benefit from swindles in the carbon markets. We can also be certain that logging companies in developing countries will bribe government officials to support their dishonest claims of having reduced emissions. Finally, indigenous people who dwell in forests will face pressures to forfeit residence on their traditional lands.

Even as REDD has yet to take off, the problems sure to be associated with it have already begun to appear. In October 2011 hundreds of huts were torched and thousands forcefully evicted from the Rufiji Delta mangrove forest in Tanzania.[58] The researchers Betsy Beymer-Farris and Thomas Bassett contend that the eviction plans were part of an effort to make the forest "REDD ready": "The removal of the Warufiji 'simplifies' the mangrove forests in order to make levels of carbon sequestration 'legible' for carbon markets."[59]

Beymer-Farris and Basset note that schemes such as REDD seek to commodify the biosphere—they amount to "subsuming ecology within the market economy."[60] This is nothing new for capitalism. To subordinate the natural environment to the needs of the market is, as Karl Polanyi points out in his discussion of land, an intrinsic feature of our economic system:

> The economic function is but one of many vital functions of land. It invests man's life with stability; it is the site of his habitation; it is a condition of his physical safety; it is the landscape and the seasons. We might as well imagine his being born without hands and feet as carrying on his life without land. And yet to separate land from man and to organize society in such a way as to satisfy the requirements of a real-estate market was a vital part of the utopian concept of a market economy.[61]

The commodification of the natural environment is an absurd exercise considering the inestimable (non-economic) value of nature. Polanyi warns that it is also dangerous. "To allow the market mechanism to be sole director of the ... natural environment" would mean certain ruin: "Nature would be reduced to its elements, neighborhoods and landscapes defiled, rivers polluted... the power to produce food and raw materials destroyed."[62] It is the logic of commodification—a logic that views the abundance offered by nature as simply a means to drive economic activity and obtain profits—

which is leading us towards catastrophe. Yet in the face of environmental collapse we are being offered intensified commodification as a solution. In the case of carbon trading and schemes like REDD, it is the very air we breathe (specifically the carbon dioxide within it) that is being commodified.

In order to protect forests from being cut down and turned into palm oil plantations or cattle ranches, we are told that the carbon dioxide they sequester must be assigned a monetary value. But tropical forests are not simply reserves of wood and containers for storing carbon dioxide. They are indescribably lush ecosystems that support the livelihoods of countless species through the functioning of numerous complementary processes. It is simply preposterous to hand over the management of forests to competing moneyed interests who, on the one hand, seek to profit from cutting them down and, on the other, want to have them be preserved in order to make a profit. The latter's driving motive is profit, not conservation, and effective oversight is all but impossible. We can therefore be certain that those looking to make a buck from preserving forests will not be troubled if the preservation is imaginary, as long as their profits are real.

FLIP THIS CAPITAL ECLIPSE

For capitalist civilization, nature is a plane to be commodified and conquered. But a societal perspective that holds the natural world to be something that can be dominated by human beings stands in stark conflict with reality. Human beings are *a part* of nature. We cannot dominate something that we are a part of, just as any group of cells that make up the body of an organism cannot dominate that organism. In their attempts to realize domination, the best result a group of cells can hope to achieve is to turn cancerous and overwhelm the organism. But this, of course, will only lead to the demise of the organism, along with which the cells themselves will perish.

We may have an extraordinary ability to mold our surroundings to our liking, but this does not separate us from the natural processes that brought us into being and continue to shape our development. Though, as a consequence of our cancerous attempts to dominate nature, our "development" is soon to become a marked regression. In order to establish an agreeable relationship with the natural world, we have to learn to live as a part of it. This means that the biosphere can no longer be regarded simply as a means to realize continuing economic growth and ever-increasing corporate profits.

The old fable of "The Frog and the Scorpion" serves as a rather neat allegory for the relationship between society and private capital. In the story, the scorpion wants to get across a river and asks the frog to give her a lift. The frog is afraid that the scorpion will sting her so she initially refuses to swim across the river with the scorpion on her back. But the scorpion comforts the frog by pointing out that if she stung her during the river-crossing they would both drown. The frog is eventually convinced by the scorpion's reasoning and they start the journey across the river. Sure enough, partway through the swim the scorpion stings the frog, incapacitating her. With her last breath the frog yells out, "Why?" To which the scorpion can only respond, "It is my nature." We have to recognize that it is in the nature of capital to risk civilizational collapse in order to secure short-term profits. We cannot change this nature, and must refuse to continue carrying it on our backs.

The way to avert the climate crisis is not a "back-to-the-wild" strategy that involves taking apart industrial civilization, as some environmentalists advocate. As romantic as such scenarios may seem, implementing them would result in massive amounts of suffering. Widespread famine, especially among that half of the world's population living in urban areas, would no doubt be an outcome.

A rationally managed industrial civilization can exist in harmony with nature. Indeed, the manifold advantages industrialization offers are necessary for sustaining bearable living standards for the seven billion people on the planet. The faults it has produced are not inherent in industrialization or technological advancement but are, rather, the outcome of mismanagement. Industrial civilization has to remain, but the way it is managed requires radical reform. If we hope to avert the climate crisis, we cannot leave irrational private capital to continue organizing the economic sphere of life, and as a result gain massive amounts of political and cultural influence.

We must radically democratize society, including the economy. What this entails, and how we can carry it out, are the topics of focus in the next and final chapter.

CHAPTER 4

The Way Forward

*Let us finally imagine, for a change, an association
of free men, working with the means of production
held in common.*

—Karl Marx[1]

In the Persian epic poem *Shahnameh* (The Book of Kings),
the demon Ahriman conjures up a snake from each of King
Zahhak's shoulders.[2] Zahhak and his retainers try various
means to destroy the snakes, but fail each time. As soon as
one of the snakes is detached from the king's body another
grows in its place. Ahriman eventually convinces Zahhak
that the best way to deal with the snakes protruding from
his shoulders is not to try to destroy them but to nurture
them by feeding each a human brain every single day.

Thus begins, according to the epic, one of the most terrifying periods in human history. Going on to rule over the land for centuries, Zahhak ceaselessly sacrifices his subjects to keep the snakes healthy, becoming all the time more tyrannical: "And despair filled all hearts, for it was as though mankind must perish to still the appetite of those snakes sprung from Evil."[3]

Sensing the building discontent of his subjects, one day Zahhak gathers the leading persons of his kingdom and demands that they sign a document declaring him a just and noble ruler. All those present obsequiously go along with the farce except for Kaveh, an old blacksmith. Kaveh raises his voice during the gathering and condemns Zahhak for murdering sixteen of his seventeen sons to feed his serpents. He also reveals that his last remaining son is a prisoner of the king and is waiting to be put to death. Fearing the upset of his plans, Zahhak decides to feign benevolence by relating kind words to Kaveh and releasing his son from prison. Kaveh, however, refuses to concede that the king's gesture of charity is sufficient atonement for his crimes. When asked again by Zahhak to sign the testimony he responds by saying: "Not so, thou wicked and ignoble man … I will not lend my hand unto this lie."[4] He then tears up the document, boldly walks out of the assembly and sets about rallying an army to help bring Zahhak's rule to an end and appoint the hero Fereydun as king.

It seems today that humankind must perish to satiate the appetite of capital. All the while, most intellectuals and activists insist that they are believers in the capitalist system —

though they may be interested in changing things for the better, they steadfastly commit to seeking only those solutions that fit within the bounds of the existing arrangement.

This is no way to create the change we need. If we are serious about making things better we must adopt Kaveh's disposition and reject the false charities and insufficient improvements allowed by the reigning system. But what system is to succeed capitalism—who, or what, will be our Fereydun? And how do we hope to achieve our objective? This chapter is devoted to discussing the kind of new social arrangement that needs to be built and the means that appear necessary for building it.

To begin with we should go over what we have covered so far about what a desirable social arrangement would look like. The petty individualism of our day would have to go. The idea of individual freedom would not have its basis in the following anti-social maxim: "You stay out of my way and I will stay out of yours." Instead, freedom would be based on the understanding that society has the ability, and indeed the obligation, to enable individuals to develop and achieve healthy desires over destructive ones. To truly be a society—one that has the legitimacy to actively shape and help achieve the desires of individuals—a collective of individuals must be democratically constituted. In a democracy, among other things, individuals would have ready access to correct and relevant information about matters that affect them.

As we have seen, capitalism is unable to deliver on any of these attributes of a desirable social arrangement. Instead of having our needs and desires shaped by a democratically constituted society, our lives are directed in significant part by unaccountable corporate power. Instead of having ready access to correct and relevant information, we are inundated with propaganda on behalf of political and economic elites. Instead of democracy (rule of the people), we have plutocracy (rule of the rich). But what do a socially-founded concept of individual freedom, a lack of propaganda, and genuine rule of the people have to do with solving the problems of global inequality and climate change?

Quite a lot, as it turns out.

POSSESSIVE VERSUS CREATIVE DESIRES

In his book *Political Ideals*, the philosopher and social activist Bertrand Russell distinguishes between two kinds of goods, both of which correspond with a particular kind of desire. There exist, on the one hand, material goods that correspond with possessive desires. On the other hand, there are intellectual and spiritual goods that correspond with creative desires. Material goods tend to have the attribute of excludability—one person's shiny new cell phone, for example, cannot also be owned by someone else. Goods corresponding with creative desires are not burdened with this divisive attribute:

> If one man knows a science, that does not prevent
> others from knowing it; on the contrary, it helps them
> to acquire the knowledge. If one man is a great artist
> or poet, that does not prevent others from painting
> pictures or writing poems, but helps to create the at-
> mosphere in which such things are possible. If one
> man is full of good-will toward others, that does not
> mean that there is less good-will to be shared among
> the rest; the more good-will one man has, the more
> he is likely to create among others. In such matters
> there is no *possession*, because there is not a definite
> amount to be shared; any increase anywhere tends
> to produce an increase everywhere.[5]

Russell maintains that the fervent desire to satisfy petty
material wants is at best a waste of time—it gets in the way
of thinking about more important things and working
to achieve more meaningful goals. At worst the desire to
continually fulfill material wants, and the pattern of thinking that it inspires, "leads to competition, envy, domination, cruelty, and almost all the moral evils that infest the
world."[6]

Possessive desires are often found at the root of conflict,
exploitation, and other associated evils. When it comes to
creative desires, however, the picture is altogether different.
Wickedness has little room to flourish among efforts to attain creative fulfillment as there is little to be gained in such
a pursuit by antagonizing and bringing harm to others.
"You may kill an artist or a thinker," Russell writes, "but

you cannot acquire his art or his thought."[7] Rather than conflict and antagonism, the natural associates of creative desires are the likes of cooperation and mutual goodwill.

Ending the exploitation that keeps much of the world's population from realizing a decent standard of living and avoiding ecological catastrophe will require making the achievement of creative desires, rather than possessive ones, the driving force behind our actions. But promoting creative desires over possessive ones is not a matter of lecturing individuals about the need to cultivate and pursue intellectual and spiritual wants. As Russell points out, it will require replacing the institutions, particularly the economic institutions, that drive us to pursue possessive desires.[8] In other words, it will require overcoming capitalism. Capitalism cannot be expected to effectively promote creative desires in place of possessive ones. It is the continuing proliferation of possessive desires that keeps the present system going.[9]

Upon hearing the suggestion that we should work to overcome capitalism, people often react by stating that seeking a radical transformation of the social order is perhaps too idealistic and that a better-regulated capitalism is a more worthwhile, more realistically achievable goal. Those who are unwilling to adopt a radical approach to activism have a habit of saying that we must "work with what we have." There is no point in building castles in the sky, they tell us; we have to stay grounded. This kind of tepid attitude relies on a grave misunderstanding of the limitations of capitalism.

While it is true that some improvements can be made within the bounds of the existing system, ultimately there can be no such thing as a democratic, socially just, and environmentally sustainable capitalism. As we have seen, capitalism unavoidably produces a mass of propaganda that makes meaningful democracy impossible; it unavoidably produces a world full of injustice and inequality in order to secure a global division of labor suitable to profit-making; and it unavoidably produces the kind of ecological destruction that makes its own longevity, and that of human civilization, impossible. Once these features of capitalism are recognized it becomes clear that it is not idealistic to seek to overcome it. It is in fact idealistic and impractical to expect capitalism to eventually become sufficiently reformed. Pragmatism is on the side of those who realize that capitalism must be overcome if we want to live in a sufficiently just world—indeed, if we want to have a world to live in at all.

Capitalism is nearing the end of its life. There can be no doubt about that. The only question is whether it will take humanity with it when it passes from the scene. We certainly have to work with what we have, but there is also the matter of how we work with it: we can either work with what we have to stall meaningful progress, or we can work with what we have to spur on the needed change.

The system that will succeed capitalism, if it is to be socially just and ecologically sustainable, will have to be one in which creative desires are more highly prized than possessive ones. It therefore follows that the new system will have to be quite a bit more democratic than our present arrangement. Without substantive democracy, our needs and desires will continue to be molded by elites who will ensure that efforts to fulfill our individual desires simultaneously forward their interests.

As discussed in the first chapter, our reliance on cars makes very little sense if we pretend that we lived in a democratic society where we came together as a collective to review the pros and cons of building urban environments that necessitate widespread car ownership. Our reliance on cars makes quite a lot of sense, however, if we realize that corporations that benefit from the widespread use of cars have played a large role in shaping our need and desire for them through use of their political and cultural power. Our desire for cars makes even more sense when we come to understand that, as noted in the third chapter, to sustain its impossible need for perpetual growth, the existing economic system requires an ever-increasing number of cars to be produced and sold.

RETHINKING DEMOCRACY

It would be useful at this point to briefly outline the blatant inadequacies of the concept of democracy as it is usually understood today. For this, the perspective held by Gandhi—a staunch democrat if there ever was one—will serve as a good starting place. Gandhi saw genuine democracy as quite a bit more than voting every few years for elite representatives who have little interest or ability to make decisions on behalf of their constituents. As a subject of the British Empire, his criticism tended to be directed at Britain's political system, but it can readily be extended to the concept of democracy as it is generally understood today.

Gandhi pointed out that "it is generally acknowledged that the members [of the British Parliament] are hypocritical and selfish. Each thinks of his own little interest." Parliament, he wrote, is "buffeted about like a prostitute" by the Prime Minister: "His energy is concentrated upon securing the success of his party. His care is not always that the Parliament shall do right. Prime Ministers are known to have made the Parliament do things merely for party advantage."[10]

Gandhi, it should be clear, held "Western democracy" to be a farce. "True democracy cannot be worked by twenty men sitting at the center," he wrote, "It has to be worked from below, by the people of every village."[11]

It is no accident that "Western democracy" has very little democratic content. The Founding Fathers of the United States, whose example would serve as an inspiration for all those who have proclaimed to uphold modern-day representative government, were a rather elitist bunch and were openly hostile to the concept of democracy.[12]

The political system favored by the Founders, and the one that they successfully put into place, was a republic, not a democracy. Thanks to the triumph of propaganda, we have come to regard the two as one and the same whereas James Madison, the "Father of the Constitution," expressly warned against "the confounding of a republic and a democracy."[13] The word "republic" comes from the Latin "respublica," which translates to "concern of the people." Throughout history this has meant that an elite few rule while the common people are allowed a marginal role in politics. In the ancient Roman Republic, for example, plebeians could register their "concern" by electing several executive magistrates from a selection of aristocrats; by electing plebeian tribunes who had little influence over politics (they were, in any case, usually closely allied with the aristocrats); and by taking up agitation against the Senate (a body made up of unelected aristocrats).

Are modern-day republics all that different? In pointing to differences one is perhaps especially tempted to note that in our time there exist much wider franchises, elected legislatures, and no legally enforced class-based requirements for holding public office. These are certainly differences in execution, but do they lead to different outcomes? Hardly. It is widely recognized, for instance, that being a class apart from common people helps a great deal in getting elected to positions of power. Nearly half of all members of the U.S. Congress are millionaires;[14] more than one in ten are among the richest 1 percent in the country.[15] (In Rome, too, by the time of the Late Republic, plebeians could stand for all public offices. This did not mean, however, that just any commoner could become a magistrate or a senator. Those who managed to do so tended to be members of what amounted to a plebeian aristocracy.)[16]

No matter what the background of our elected officials may be, they have to court those who possess inordinate amounts of wealth. It is no secret that the people's "representatives" are beholden much more to the moneyed interests in society than they are to those who vote for them. This becomes most obvious when the issue of campaign contributions is probed. As David Graeber notes,

> the average senator or congressman in Washington needs to raise roughly $10,000 a week from the time they take office if they expect to be reelected—money that they raise almost exclusively from the wealthiest 1 percent. As a result, elected officials spend an estimated 30 percent of their time soliciting bribes.[17]

That the bribes are recognized as legal is not a heartening piece of information. It only means that legalized "bribery has become the very basis of [the American] system of government."[18] In India, which often finds itself described as "the world's largest democracy," activists have taken up the following song to highlight the dismal reality of the political system in their country:

> Look at the politician setting off for Delhi
> He'll forget the slum and the alley
> The politician in handspun cotton
> Folds his hands and asks for votes
> He wins, becomes a bigshot
> Then strangulates his voters

> Look at the politician setting off for Delhi
> He'll forget the slum, the alley
> For his election expenses he takes favors from the rich
> Raises prices, encourages Black money
> Look at the politician on his way to Delhi
> He'll be back in five years
> Fold his hands, ask for votes
> Empower his yes men and make fools of us[19]

Even in countries where money does not so transparently drive politics, the wealthy invariably command overwhelming amounts of influence. One important way this is ensured, as we have repeatedly seen, is through the media's willingness to skirt the truth to instead propagate the views of the powerful.

The fact that democracy has come to be associated with elections is simply tragic. Elections, Graeber points out, have traditionally been a characteristic of aristocratic—rather than democratic—forms of government.[20] Those from the upper classes, regarded as intrinsically superior to commoners (of better "stock," as it were), contested elections for public office. It is easy enough to imagine noblemen mobilizing their resources in a paternalistic manner to expand the size of their respective factions and win votes.[21]

In democracies, rather than elections, lottery systems have been the norm. Anyone meeting the agreed upon basic standard for holding a particular position could volunteer for it and would have an equal chance of being selected as any other volunteer. Doing things this way guards against the inherent factionalism of elections from cropping up.[22]

The word "democracy," of course, comes from the Greek "demokratia," meaning "rule of the people." As opposed to the spectator role allotted to the common people in a republic, democracy places them at the center of the action. It involves people coming together to consider, discuss, and make decisions about matters that affect them.

Democracy cannot be reduced to simply counting votes, or "majority rule." Majority voting has certainly been used to make decisions in *some* democratic arrangements—most famously in ancient Athens. However, in *most* cases throughout history—including, for instance, among many Amerindian nations—instead of relying on voting to reach decisions, democratic assemblies have sought to achieve synthesis, compromise, and consensus.[23] Whatever the particular process employed, the basic principle guiding democracy is the idea that those who will be affected by a decision have an equal right to participate in crafting it.

When arrangements of this kind are discussed today they are often referred to as "participatory democracy." But this is a redundant phrase; democracy is either participatory or it is not democracy. That is to say, the people can hardly govern themselves if they are not participating in their government.

The establishment of democracy would lead to the radical change of our political institutions. The state as it exists today would certainly not make it through the transition. Decision-making would be decentralized to the extent that is possible. Federations would have to be created among several localities to manage regional and inter-regional affairs. Delegates would be selected to speak on behalf of localities and sit on committees that manage specific affairs—along with other safeguards, those appointed to such positions would rotate often and be subject to easy recall by citizens. In this way, an arrangement could be brought about along the lines envisioned by Gandhi: "worked from below, by the people of every village."

It is important to note that this vision cannot be realized if the existing economic arrangement remains as it is. Our economic activity, which is in large part managed by unaccountable corporate power, must also be democratized. Any political system, no matter how it was arranged, would be forced to bend to the will of the existing economic elite if their power was left untouched.

Therefore, to truly establish a democratic social arrangement we would want to establish socialism.

THE MEANING OF SOCIALISM

Socialism is a much abused word in our day. It can stand for quite a few different things in the minds of people, but rarely does it stand for what is actually meant by the word. Upon being brought up in polite company, it commonly evokes refutation through reflexive reference to totalitarianism and the Soviet Union. Interestingly enough, whenever it is associated with totalitarianism, mention of "Big Brother" and "Newspeak" have an easy time finding themselves in the mix of charges laid against socialism.

The use of George Orwell's work to refute socialism is rather ironic because Orwell was an out-an-out socialist. He relates the following in his essay "Why I Write": "Every line of serious work that I have written since 1936 has been written, directly or indirectly, against totalitarianism and for democratic socialism, as I understand it."[24] Needless to say, the recasting of Orwell as something of an anti-socialist champion is yet another example of the triumph of propaganda in our time. This association has become acceptable, as Noam Chomsky notes, because of the propaganda efforts of both the Soviet Union and the West during the Cold War.

As with Orwell and anti-socialism, associating socialism with the Soviet Union is a mistaken exercise. This association has become acceptable, as Noam Chomsky notes, because of the propaganda efforts of both the Soviet Union and the West during the Cold War.[25] The idea of socialism was, and continues to be, held in high esteem by poor and working people around the world. The Soviet Union wanted to associate itself with this esteem and so it described itself as socialist. For their part, Western countries described the Soviet Union as socialist in order to disparage the idea of socialism. Western propaganda claimed that socialism was authoritarianism. And if the only alternative to the capitalist order was the kind of authoritarianism that the Soviet Union represented, trying to overcome capitalism was not a good idea.

There have also been efforts made to reform the idea of socialism to make it fit within the bounds of the existing social arrangement. It is often claimed, for example, that socialism simply means rigorous involvement of the state in the existing economy. "In every country in the world," Orwell noted, "a huge tribe of party-hacks and sleek little professors are busy 'proving' that Socialism means no more than a planned state-capitalism with the grab-motive left intact."[27] When characterized in this way socialism is not always presented as a vilified concept. Regardless, this is *not* socialism.

Socialism means, to begin with, democratic management of workplaces and the wider economy. It entails the creation of, as Michael Lebowitz calls it, a "solidarian society." Lebowitz explains that economic activity within capitalism is carried out by separating human beings from other human beings. When the economy functions on the basis of individual self-interest we do not relate to each other as members of the human family but as "separate property owners."[28] In such a setting if an individual produces a good that someone else needs she does so not for the other person but for herself. She knows that her own needs will only be met if she exchanges what she can produce for what others produce. But since self-interest is what motivates us, the exchange process is rife with deception and distrust – we each try to get the best out of the deal for ourselves.

Lebowitz stresses that the way in which a society organizes its economic activity determines not only how material goods will be produced and distributed but also, because our activity makes us who we are, what kind of human beings will be produced. Since the starting point of the capitalist economy is the separation of human beings from each other, and the process throughout keeps us separated, human beings that are atomized and alienated are ultimately produced.[29]

Regarding each other as separate property owners means that if I have a need that someone else can fulfill that person has power over me. Similarly, if others have needs that I can fulfill this gives me power over them. In such a setting, where needs are seen as a mark of weakness, it becomes an embarrassment for us to point out the fact that we have needs. We are thus forced to rely on the process of market exchange, and the values that it induces in us, to hold on to dignity.[30] I will give you this, we say, if you give me that.

In a solidarian society, if you have a need that I can fulfill, rather than seeing this as an opportunity to seek advantage for myself, I will want to help you. But, it may be asked, how would any work get done in such a society? If not by the prospect of material gain, then how will individuals be driven? We have come to regard the idea that human beings are mainly, if not solely, driven by material self-interest as so self-evidently the truth that anything else appears unnatural. This surety, however, does not exist because of our profound understanding of human nature. Rather, it is a result of enculturation – a product of the age of individualism. A survey of the historical record reveals that economic systems based upon motives other than material gain are the norm. The present way of organizing society is an aberration. As Karl Polanyi explains:

> The outstanding discovery of recent historical and anthropological research is that man's economy, as a rule, is submerged in his social relationships. He does not act so as to safeguard his individual interest in the possession of material goods; he acts so as to safeguard his social standing, his social claims, his social assets. He values material goods only in so far as they serve this end. Neither the process of production nor that of distribution is linked to specific economic interests attached to the possession of goods; but every single step in that process is geared to a number of social interests which eventually ensure that the required step be taken. These interests will be very different in a small hunting or fishing community from those in a vast despotic society, but in either case the economic system will be run on noneconomic motives.[31]

Standing in stark contrast to pre-capitalist societies in which economic activity was "run on noneconomic motives," the all-encompassing market that characterized capitalism would for the first time coordinate the production and distribution of goods on the basis of material self-interest. The market would be the institution that signaled the coming about of an economic sphere distinct from the social relations that characterized wider society. This was a significant break from the past—"normally, the economic order is merely a function of the social, in which it is contained."[32]

Society itself would be thoroughly forced to change in order to accommodate the all-encompassing market. Notably, labor and land would henceforth be regarded as commodities, to be bought and sold as anything else in the marketplace. "But labor and land are no other than the human beings themselves of which every society consists and the natural surroundings in which it exists. To include them in the market mechanism means to subordinate the substance of society itself to the laws of the market."[33] Therefore, for capitalism to function, society "had [to] become an accessory of the economic system."[34]

Socialism would entail an end to the existence of a distinct area of life regarded as the economic sphere. The democratic management of economic life would mean that the economy would become subordinate to the wider relationships that make up society. Noneconomic motives would direct economic activity, as they have throughout most of human history. Building a solidarian society based

on social ownership and democratic management of production and distribution will mean the achievement of
"the real purpose of socialism," as Albert Einstein saw it:
"to overcome and advance beyond the predatory phase of
human development."[35]

The vast amounts of scientific knowledge possessed by
our civilization can then properly be put to use to end the
crippling poverty that needlessly afflicts countless millions around the world. The cautious use of resources and
discharge of pollution can ensure that the well-being of
coming generations of life is safeguarded. And a focus on
cultivating creative desires can unlock human potential.

TRANSFORMATION

We cannot, as some argue, wait around for capitalism to
collapse and then set about building a freer, more just,
world. Even if capitalism crumbles away before completely devastating the environment—of which there is little
guarantee—the social consequences of such a collapse
would lead to untold suffering, and would quite likely result in the coming about of a less free, less just, social order
than the one currently in existence. This is because chaotic
settings do not often serve as good backdrops for mobilizing people—the amount of energy required to achieve
self-preservation becomes too great. At the same time,
such settings make great playgrounds for the cruel and
ruthless, allowing them to achieve domination over the

meek and humble. We must, therefore, struggle to over-come capitalism while it continues to reign.

To achieve this transformation we need to struggle to build new, and expand the scope and effectiveness of existing, democratic institutions. Not only do we need to enhance the limited democracy that currently resides in the state, we have to build community and workers' councils that together can provide a basis for a social arrangement that eclipses capitalism. The state must be made increasingly transparent and accountable—its workings made clearer and more accessible to the public it purports to represent. Community and workers' councils must at the same time begin to encroach on the space currently occupied by the state and private capital.

The exact sequence of events, and the events themselves, through which the needed change comes about will no doubt differ from place to place. The conditions that exist in any given country will require a strategy specific to them. The pace, too, will vary from location to location. In some places, the process of change may be gradual. In others, it may involve powerful ruptures that force change to take place, despite the dams built to hold it back. Though, in all cases it is likely that a mix of both gradualism and powerful ruptures will help us build from victory to victory. In all cases, there will be periods of stagnation as well as setbacks. The inertia that keeps the existing system in motion will itself be difficult to confront, but in addition to this inertia there will be ceaseless attempts by capital and state power to try to undermine our efforts.

Power will not sit idly by and let us go about our work. It will especially not, as some seem to think, assist us in building the world anew. Any challenge to it will be met with repression. Perhaps most prominently, power will rely on the media to spread propaganda on its behalf. Despite the importance of our work and despite the resonance it may have among the wider public, the media will ignore us when it is possible and deemed necessary to do so. When it is no longer possible to ignore us, the media will do all it can to mock, disparage, and vilify us. In addition to propaganda, far more sinister means will be employed to ensure that emancipatory projects do not succeed. These include intimidation, arrests, assassinations, coups, economic strangulation, and military intervention.

The harshest of these measures are of course reserved for use in the Global South where it becomes perfectly clear, as Gandhi noted, that "Western democracy" serves as "merely a cloak to hide the Nazi and the Fascist tendencies of imperialism." Those of us who live in the Global North must struggle to ensure that repression and exploitation in the South cannot be carried out or given support by our governments. In doing so we can help give concrete form to the spirit of solidarity required to achieve the global change we need.

Whereas the worldwide scope of our task may seem daunting, in a way the massive scope is a good thing: the wider the size of the overall struggle, the greater scope there is for the numerous smaller struggles of which it is comprised to have points of interdependence and the greater amount of mutual support and learning we can obtain from each other as we press ahead.

Points of contact between the smaller struggles, as well as the relationship between smaller struggles and the overall fight, are the keys to making contributions to what may seem like a goal that is impossible to contribute to. The idea of upending an entire social system and replacing it with another seems, to be sure, like a superhuman task if it is looked upon only from this broad view. Once it is realized, however, that there are many smaller, easier to grasp, struggles to which energy can be applied in order to make a contribution to the larger struggle of overcoming capitalism, it becomes quite a bit easier to find a place to begin. It is important, however, that the smaller struggles not remain isolated. They must be taken up with the aim of helping them achieve coalescence so that the ultimate goal—complete social transformation—can be achieved.

A great example of this approach is provided by Martin Luther King, Jr. While he is remembered mainly for his activism relating to racial equality, King's interests and goals were far grander. He understood that the issue of race was securely connected with other important matters relating to justice. These various issues could only really be understood and dealt with if they were looked at in relation to each other as well as the wider context in which they existed.

Real progress was much more likely to be forthcoming if the various connecting pieces were collected together and their common roots were laid bare. This is why, along with struggling for racial equality, King was an opponent of the Vietnam War as well as a staunch advocate for the rights of workers and the destitute. He took a stand against, as he referred to them, "the giant triplets of racism, extreme materialism, and militarism."[36] When he decided to speak out against the war many of his allies, King reported, were not pleased: "'Peace and civil rights don't mix,' they say."[37] For King, there were obvious connections between them.

He pointed out that Black soldiers were dying in disproportionate numbers in Vietnam.[38] Those who could not obtain a decent livelihood at home were being subjected to even greater hardship by being sent to fight and die in scores in a foreign land. And how ironic it was that young Black men, "who had been crippled by society," were fighting to "guarantee liberties in Southeast Asia which they had not found in Southwest Georgia and East Harlem." Whereas Blacks and whites could be found working side-by-side in "brutal solidarity" to oppress the Vietnamese, for some strange reason they were expressly segregated in the neighbourhoods and schools throughout much of the U.S.[39]

King also lamented the difference between the seemingly limitless resources available to fight the war and the pitiful amounts reserved to deal with the problems of poverty at home. It was clear "that America would never invest the necessary funds or energies in rehabilitation of its poor so long as adventures like Vietnam continued to draw men and skills and money, like some demonic, destructive suction tube."[40] Of course, when it came to the issue of economic exploitation and poverty, King's concern for it was not restricted to the U.S. He expressly denounced the "capitalists of the West investing huge sums of money in Asia, Africa, and South America, only to take the profits out with no concern for the social betterment of the countries."[41]

King understood that the common roots of these problems were the structures of capitalism. Therefore, to properly push forward the cause of justice, a complete transformation of the social order was needed. A "radical revolution of values" was necessary: "We must rapidly begin the shift from a thing-oriented society to a person-oriented society."[42] King envisioned that this could be done by working to develop small struggles until they were able to break out of their bounds and take a grander form. Accordingly, he saw the civil rights movement as a building challenge to the existing economic system:

> The Negro revolt is evolving into more than a quest for desegregation and equality. It is a challenge to a system that has created miracles of production and technology to create justice. If humanism is locked outside the system, Negroes will have revealed its inner core of despotism and a far greater struggle for liberation will unfold.[43]

In the final years of his life King sought to expand out of his mold as solely an advocate for civil rights, make common cause with the anti-war effort and the workers' movement, and help these struggles to coalesce and become a foundation for the wider struggle to bring about a "radical redistribution of economic power."[44]

Had he refrained from discussing U.S. imperialism his reputation certainly would have been better off for it. The American media, King related, "will praise you when you say, 'Be non-violent toward [segregationists] Bull Connor and Jim Clark in Alabama,' but will curse and damn you when you say, 'Be non-violent toward little brown Vietnamese children.'"[45]

But King realized that remaining an advocate for civil rights and not speaking out against the war would involve giving into a blatant moral inconsistency while also not serving to be as effective a path for creating the kind of society-wide change that he regarded as necessary. He therefore rejected the approach chosen by many of his erstwhile allies who wanted to retain the favor of the media and the powerful. This same dejected approach is today often taken up within the NGO community whose members have segmented themselves into niches—some concern themselves strictly with specific issues relating to poverty, others the environment, etc.—and like to pretend that the issues they are concerned with exist in a moral and material vacuum. We must reject this weak-kneed way to conduct activism if our efforts are going to coalesce into a mass movement that can take on the challenge of transforming society.

The mass movement we need to bring into being will be quite like the army raised by Kaveh in certain ways: it will be composed of large numbers of everyday citizens and have the support of the vast majority of citizens who are not themselves able to take an active role in the movement. Of course, the movement will not be like Kaveh's army in that it will not be an army of troops trained and regimented for combat. As King saw it, the mass movement was to take the form of a sustained campaign of non-violent civil disobedience. This remains an appropriate model for us today. The civil disobedience campaign can flout laws and convention by, among other things, occupying public spaces, disrupting socially and ecologically destructive economic activity (such as weapons manufacturing and oil production), taking over workplaces to achieve workers control, creating links between different parts of the movement, and organizing democratic decision-making bodies like community and workers' councils that can replace existing authority.

What about capturing state power? Should getting a political party allied to the movement elected to power be a goal of the movement? In considering this potential route we must be wary of the many problems that will undoubtedly accompany it. Everyone is well aware of the dulling effects of party politics and statecraft: the election cycles, which capture people's attention for short periods of time only to ensure they will return to apathy; the excessive amounts of media attention given to trivialities; the coached politicians who talk for so long but say very little;

the senseless appeals to nationalism; and the professional-ized state bureaucracy that seems to take life and vigor out of everything it touches.

Trudging through all of this must not take the place of building and sustaining the mass movement. If a party hopes to represent and remain accountable to the move-ment, the movement must not only exist but be thriving. The movement, therefore, is of primary importance even when considering the capture of state power.

Where state power can be captured, it may be able to help us to more effectively take on capital and force it to deliver concessions, while also helping to expand the scope of new democratic forms of decision-making beyond com-munities and workplaces by linking them together. The movement will have to make demands to the state, no matter who controls its machinery. These demands will be more readily carried out if state power is in the hands of those allied with the movement. But in such cases the movement must not allow itself to be coopted by the state or dissipate. It must be sustained and it must remain an autonomous force.

Whereas a friendly party with control of the state can be of help in constructing the new social order, it is the work of the mass movement that will be most important to building this order. The movement must create the institu-tions that will replace those that currently exist. More im-portantly, it is through involvement within the movement that the new citizen will be born. Indeed, the new human being—whose sensibilities are not stamped by the age of individualism.

Finally, activist culture today happens to be rooted in the notion that people must be given *something to do*; they must have an *action they can take*—sign a petition, write a letter, attend a demonstration. While action is a necessity, activists must look to begin their work at a much more fundamental level. We must give people *something to think about*—*something to believe in*. What people go on to do will be, as a result, more earnest and sustained. As Peter Kropotkin observed, "The bold thought first, and the bold deed will not fail to follow."[46]

Afterword

I began writing *Confronting Injustice* during the last year of my life as an undergraduate student. Most of my friends had left town by then. I had stuck around to take some extra courses that I thought would help me get into graduate school. Taking extra time to finish off my degree and not having many friends around gave me a fair bit of space to reflect on the chapter that was closing in my life.

The most memorable part of my time at university had been the activism I was involved in. Through the years, I was able to take part in a large variety of initiatives. I helped raise money for charitable causes, hosted letter-writing campaigns, encouraged the purchase of fair-trade coffee on campus, took part in public demonstrations, wrote articles for student newspapers, organized book clubs, and lots else.

As a result of my involvement in activism, I found that I was consistently growing as a person. Much of this growth, funnily enough, was in the form of transcending the activist outlook that I had at any particular time. Being involved in different types of initiatives allowed me to compare and contrast them, and try to identify their respective limitations.

When I came up with the idea of writing a book, I decided on two justifications to convince myself that it would be a useful way to spend my time. First, taking on a book-writing project would allow me to clarify my thoughts and give a coherent shape to the political outlook that had been forming in my mind. Second, I would be able to engage my activist friends in a detailed manner with the ideas I had about the limitations of the initiatives we were involved in.

In retrospect, the first of these justifications came to be realized quite a bit more resoundingly than I had anticipated. The process of writing a book was a lot more rewarding, from the point of view of my own intellectual and political development, than I had originally thought it would be. The second justification was not as decisively realized. Reading was not a particularly popular pastime in the activist circles I was a part of. For some reason, I had expected that knowing someone who had written a book would get people to at least read that particular book. Not everyone I had wanted to engage with ended up reading *Confronting Injustice*, though everyone I knew was overwhelmingly supportive of the project.

Among my initial reasons for writing a book, the possibility that people I did not know would read it was not included. I did not, of course, completely discount the possibility. In fact, I wrote the book in a way that I thought would be accessible and relevant to the experience of a wide range of activists. But I had reasoned that even if the book did not attract a readership outside of the activist circles I was a part of, writing it would still be a worthwhile effort.

I decided to self-publish *Confronting Injustice*, which meant that its distribution would be limited. Despite this, it ended up making its way, through word of mouth and other means, to unexpectedly distant places. By no means did the book attract a large audience, but it was heartening to receive occasional messages from strangers across the continent who said they had enjoyed reading it. These messages, as well as encouragement from friends, helped to convince me that the book deserved to have a life in the hands of a real publisher.

The Haymarket Books edition, coming two years after its initial publication, gives me a chance to revisit the politics and ideas presented in *Confronting Injustice* with fresh eyes. I am happy to report that these politics and ideas are, on the whole, still with me, though the distance of two years has inevitably meant that they have become sharpened in some places, become less strident in others, and have in certain instances come to be altered.

This afterword allows me to 1) fill in an important gap, and 2) discuss a noteworthy alteration in my point of view. The following two sections are arranged precisely in that order.

The first section deals with the kind of activism variously referred to as "anti-oppression," "privilege politics," "identity politics," and so on. This approach to activism has acquired broad appeal. Despite that appeal, I missed dealing with it when I originally wrote *Confronting Injustice*. Here, I briefly try to demonstrate that the outlook and concepts this approach promotes tend to be individualistic, confused, and unhelpful.

The second section discusses the need for activists to think beyond the grassroots. One critique of *Confronting Injustice* that has convinced me is that it seemed to uncritically champion grassroots organizing. I argue below that grassroots organizing on its own will not bring about the widespread changes that are needed. Active efforts to capture political power will be necessary. We therefore have to look to organizational forms that can help us contend for power.

FILLING A GAP

The feminist writer Gloria Jean Watkins, who uses the pen name "bell hooks," is a popular figure among activists who espouse the politics of anti-oppression, privilege, and identity. hooks is commonly quoted on activist blogs and social media websites, on such far-ranging topics as education and Beyoncé's fashion choices. She can help provide us a window into what this kind of activism is about.

In *Feminism Is for Everybody*, hooks describes herself as "radical a feminist as one can be."[1] Phrases like "imperialist white supremacist capitalist patriarchy" are littered everywhere throughout the book. As we are about to see, hooks does not attach very much meaning to the terms she uses. These terms seem to signify nothing for her beyond allowing her to sound radical.

Most of the book is a repetitious stream of platitudes about such things as the need to overcome patriarchy, defend reproductive rights for women, do feminist consciousness-raising, with lots of radical-sounding language thrown in for effect. hooks rarely gets around to talking about anything concrete. The few times concrete things are discussed, they reveal the superficial nature of her convictions.

For instance, hooks notes that at a certain point during her time as a feminist activist, the issue of hiring domestic help came up for debate. She tells us that this was an issue of concern for "mostly white women with class privilege" who wanted to ensure that they did not "participate in the sub-ordination and dehumanization of less-privileged women." According to her, the problem was addressed as follows:

> Some of those women successfully created posi-tive bonding between themselves and the women they hired so that there could be mutual advance-ment in a larger context of inequality. Rather than abandoning the vision of sisterhood, because they could not attain some utopian state, they created a real sisterhood, one that took into account the needs of everyone involved. This was the hard work of feminist solidarity between women.[2]

As with much of her writing, it is not clear what hooks means by any of this. What does come across is that hooks does not mind the continued existence of structural in-equalities as long as there is "positive bonding" taking place between the parties involved, whatever the "positive bonding" might amount to. hooks does not seem to under-stand that *all* cases of structural inequality are justified on the basis that they lead to "mutual advancement." Wheth-er it is the inequality between men and women, between landlord and serf, between colonizer and colonized, it has always been argued that the prevailing structures "took into account the needs of everyone involved."

Whereas throughout her book hooks is adamant that she wants to overturn the existing oppressive structures, in the above quoted passage she seems to dismiss such efforts as "utopian." We learn from her that one should make peace with the prevailing arrangement. So much for her being as "radical a feminist as one can be."

Elsewhere in the book, hooks outlines the travails, in the early days of the feminist movement, of trying to get the fashion industry to cater to the needs of those with non-conformist tastes in attire: "Women had to demand that the fashion industry (which was totally male-dominated in those days) create diverse styles of clothing."[3] hooks tells us that as a result of the efforts of feminists, some of whom ended up joining the fashion industry, the industry did end up changing. But she worries that, in recent times, the victories are being rolled back.

The feminist movement, according to hooks, has not been as vigilant as it should have been. The fashion industry is once again coming to be dominated by males, and it is once again setting sexist standards of beauty. Feminist portrayals of beauty, on the other hand, are consistently being sidelined. hooks points the way forward: "Until feminists go back to the beauty industry, go back to fashion, and create an ongoing, sustained revolution, we will not be free. We will not know how to love our bodies as ourselves."[4] What a grand vision of freedom!

We just have to make sure that enough feminist designers and writers become a part of the fashion industry, and all will be set right. There is apparently nothing wrong with the fashion industry aside from its inclination to promote sexist ideals of beauty. Despite her supposed concern about the "imperialist white supremacist capitalist patriarchy," hooks appears to be unaware that the fashion industry is a leading agent of racist, sexist, capitalist exploitation around the world.

Anyone with the slightest concern for women's rights should be alert to the fact that the global trade in garments has its basis in the poorly paid labor of women from across the Third World. Over the past several decades, firms have relocated garment manufacturing to poor countries in order to benefit from lower wages and lax safety, environmental, and worker protection standards. For their part, many poor countries have been forced to attract investments from the garment industry so that they can service their debts with the export earnings. The outcome for women has not been heartening.

The garment sector in Bangladesh is a characteristic example. Women make up the majority of workers in the sector. Garment factory owners actively seek to hire women because they command lower wages relative to men. A stretch of eleven to twelve hours, with a total of fifteen minutes of break time, is a normal workday. As Peter Custers notes, when factory owners accept large orders under a short deadline, the length of the workday can become much longer: "There are instances where women workers have to toil 48, 72, or even more hours at a time."[5]

Having worked overtime, workers may find that factory owners will withhold the extra pay that they have earned. Various other abuses of this sort are commonplace.

Factory owners often refuse to adhere to basic safety standards, a result of which is that electrical fires break out in garment factories across Bangladesh on a routine basis. Safety violations in other instances can lead to the collapse of buildings in which garment manufacturing is taking place, as happened in April 2013 when the collapse of a building led to the deaths more than a thousand people. The women working for a pittance in this industry are doing so with the risk of death hanging over them.

Women workers walking to and from work, often before or after daylight, routinely face harassment, which can at times take the form of physical and sexual assault. Such risks do not disappear while the women are at work. As Custers points out:

> Sexual oppression inside the factory can take the form of sexual harassments by male supervisors and, worse, the attempt by owners to turn women into prostitutes. The latter practice is not unique to the Bangladeshi garments sector, but appears to be organized in a specific manner. A garment owner generally does not use the factory premises for sexual exploitation, but will try to lure a girl he considers beautiful into accompanying him to a hotel. The girl is called to the owner's office

and offered sweets and money in exchange for an agreement to be prostituted. In case she refuses, the woman worker, reportedly, will be dismissed from her job. Her refusal to be prostituted is punished, and treated as an act of insubordination and indiscipline.[6]

hooks has nothing to say about the young women of colour laboring to produce the diverse styles of clothing she cares so much about. In a chapter titled "Global Feminism," among other tokenistic ramblings, one can find reference to an exhortation to "decolonize feminist thinking and practice."[7] But, as one comes to expect from hooks, these are nothing but hollow words.

People like hooks have helped to create a political culture in which the use of radical-sounding language has come to replace actual radical politics. One does not have to know what anything means as long as one knows which words to use. Repetition of specific buzzwords passes for substantive discussion. And whereas the terms being repeatedly deployed—*capitalism, patriarchy, white supremacy, decolonization*, and so on—once had political significance, they now seem to only find meaning, if they have any meaning at all, in the individualized and interpersonal sense.

So capitalism has come to refer to the culture of consumerism, rather than being seen as a social system dominated by the private drive for profit. We are told that the way to combat capitalism is to refuse to shop at Walmart, to support local businesses instead, to grow our own food, and to take part in the "sharing economy." The purported solution to sexism and racism is to acknowledge, on every possible occasion, one's gender and racial privilege and to make sure that one's personal interactions with women and people of color are not tainted by prejudice. What any of this has to do with addressing the impoverishment and environmental destruction capitalism creates is not clear to me. And what it has to do with ending racism and sexism (including the racist and sexist global division of labor that is an inherent part of our social system) is also not apparent.

AN ALTERED POSITION

During the summer of 2014, I became involved in an anti-pipeline campaign in Toronto. Part of this campaign involved occupying worksites. I myself was able to take part in two such occupations. The first resulted in a one-day stoppage of work. The second stopped work for at least two days and resulted in work equipment being carried offsite. The occupations were in part meant to serve as precursors for larger actions to come, allowing the activists involved to build links and gain experience.

The campaign involved dozens of committed activists. Many other tactics aside from the occupations were used, including pressuring politicians, hosting public education events, and getting the media to cover the issue. The delays caused by the campaign reportedly resulted in costs amounting to $100 million to the pipeline company.[8] But the project remained on course. Moreover, the wider goal of drastically reducing our reliance on fossil fuels was not nearer in sight.

Involvement in the anti-pipeline campaign helped me to see that while we were good at organizing efforts against particularly harmful projects and initiatives, we did not have a broader strategy for seeking change. During the occupations I took part in, in thinking about what we were up to, much of the time my thoughts were on a part of Howard Zinn's *You Can't Be Neutral on a Moving Train*. In the autobiographical book, Zinn writes about becoming involved in a large antiwar demonstration in 1971 in Washington, DC. The twenty thousand protesters who were present gave themselves the task of "shutting down the city." The protestors broke themselves up into affinity groups, each deciding its own method of contributing to the goal: "The idea was to avoid centralized, bureaucratic organization."

As part of one affinity group, Zinn, along with Noam Chomsky, Daniel Ellsberg, and several other unlikely candidates for the activity, played a game of cat and mouse with police while trying to stop traffic. Reflecting on what they managed to achieve that day, Zinn wrote: "Truth is, symbolic actions (we were not accomplishing anything by blocking the street) always feel a little bit bizarre."[9] Anyone who has taken part in demonstrations, blockades, and occupations has at times surely been confronted with similar feelings.

I was also thinking about Gandhism during the occupations. Direct action of the kind we were engaged in has come to be closely associated with the legacy of the wise Mahatma.[10] As is well known, Gandhi's efforts to win India's independence from Britain often took the form of nonviolent civil disobedience, of which the 1930 Salt March is perhaps the most widely known example.

By contrast, little known or talked about are his (likely more important) efforts to shape the Indian National Congress into a political party that could lead the country to independence and be prepared to govern it afterwards. Gandhi, writes the historian Perry Anderson, "was a first-class organizer and fund-raiser—diligent, efficient, meticulous—who rebuilt Congress from top to bottom, endowing it with a permanent executive at national level, vernacular units at provincial level, local bases at district level, and delegates proportionate to population, not to speak of an ample treasury."[11] Crucial to Gandhi's program of reforming Congress was its transformation from a party of Indian liberal elites into one that was in touch with the masses.

About the misgivings one should have of what Congress was (and especially what it would turn into), a considerable amount could be said.[12] But without Congress, or something like it, independence for India would not have been forthcoming. The campaigns of mass civil disobedience led by Gandhi would not have been able to secure freedom on their own. Congress provided a forum to have debates and discussions, attract and produce leaders, fashion collective positions on issues of concern, and vie for increasing amounts of influence and power.

The role of Congress in the struggle for Indian independence is an important consideration in a time like ours, when all we seem to have on hand in fighting for change (particularly in the case of North America) are marches, demonstrations, blockades, and occupations, sprinkled in among always-ongoing public education efforts.

Our situation is in many ways very different from the India of Gandhi's time. India was then an underdeveloped country under the direct colonial rule of a geographically far-off nation. We in North America today live in the wealthiest societies that have ever existed and are trying to overcome oppressions that do not have as clearly obvious solutions as kicking out a far-off occupying power. Differences such as these should make it clear that we cannot simply copy the approaches that worked in a particular place at a particular time. But by no means can we completely disregard the lessons of past struggles. One of these lessons, surely, is that political parties are important.

The revolutionary writer and artist William Morris once proclaimed that "if our ideas of a new Society are anything more than a dream ... three qualities must animate the due effective majority of the working people; and then, I say, the thing will be done." The three qualities Morris had in mind were "intelligence enough to conceive, courage enough to will, and power enough to compel."[13] The last of these, power enough to compel, hardly ever seems to be a consideration of activists today. The fact that power, and indeed *compulsion*, will be required to reorder society seems a wholly suspect idea to us.

Power: that is the thing that the people in charge have, is it not? And will we not be just like them if we were to have it? All of this tepidness about power is not helped by the fact that we live in a time when practically anything that could involve centralization and hierarchy is equated with elitist vanguardism. The fact remains, however, whatever the antihierarchical, anticentralization, and anticompulsion biases of modern activism may be, we are going to have to take power in order to get done what we need to get done.

Ultimately, we have to overcome the workshop and protest models of activism that have become entrenched in our time. Rather than continuing to just rely on sporadic flare-ups to create change, we are called on to work with institutional forms that can deliver protracted challenges to the status quo in pushing for progressive change. This point, it should perhaps be emphasized, is the crux of my altered position. A multitude of local, grassroots efforts will not come together on their own to create a greater whole. We have to create organizational formations that can help to coordinate such efforts across geographical space and over long periods of time.

Protests, marches, and direct actions need not to be put on hold, but they do need to be supplemented with organization building. One thing we learn from past efforts to build mass, democratic political parties is that such things take time. The urgency of the environmental crisis perhaps makes us unwilling to put energy into efforts that have long gestation periods. There does not seem to be a way around it, however. We are just going to have to commit to being in this for the long, slow haul.

Notes

INTRODUCTION

1   Kurt Vonnegut, *Slaughterhouse-five; or, The Children's Crusade: A Duty-Dance with Death* (New York: Delacorte Press, 1969), 9.

2   Jane Qui, "Tibetan Glaciers Shrinking Rapidly," *Nature*, July 15, 2012.

3   The building competition over the resources and waterways of the Arctic and the fate of the Nile are other examples.

4   Claire Provost, "Environmental threats could push billions into extreme poverty, warns UN," *Guardian*, March 14, 2013.

5   Vonnegut, *Slaughterhouse-five*, 188.

6   Edward Wong, "Air Pollution Linked to 1.2 Million Premature Deaths in China," *New York Times*, April 1, 2013.

7   Jonathan Kaiman, "Chinese environment official challenged to swim in polluted river," *Guardian*, February 21, 2013.

8   John Vidal and David Adam, "China overtakes US as world's biggest CO2 emitter," *Guardian,* 19 June 2007, Web.

9   Fred Magdoff and John Bellamy Foster, *What Every Environ-mentalist Needs to Know About Capitalism* (New York: Month-ly Review Press, 2011), 33.

10   Quoted in ibid.

11   Johan Galtung, "A World in Economic Crisis," (Working Paper No. 111, 2002), Retrieved from http://vbn.aau.dk/files/33749141/DIR_wp_111.pdf, 3.

12   Charles I. Burch, "Oil Companies Discover 'Sustainability'," *AlterNet*, July 29, 2005.

13   See the December 15, 2009 press release titled "Nestlé Wa-ters North America Continues Plastic Reduction Efforts with New, Lighter Bottle" on nestle-watersna.com.

14   Brian K. Murphy, "International NGOs and the Challenge of Modernity," *Development in Practice* 10.3–4 (2000): 330–47, 343. Murphy goes on to add: "What the corporate PR man-ager understands implicitly as economic propaganda, NGO people often repeat as articles of faith" (344).

CHAPTER 1: THE AGE OF INDIVIDUALISM

1   Eduardo Galeano, *The Book of Embraces* (New York: W.W. Norton, 1991), 123.

2   From a talk delivered at York University on March 10, 2010. It is available to be viewed online on tvo.org under the ti-tle "Palagummi Sainath on the Age of Inequality." Accessed July 21, 2013.

3   This is, in essence, the liberal conception of freedom — artic-ulated most famously by John Stuart Mill as follows: "The only freedom which deserves the name is that of pursuing our own good in our own way, so long as we do not attempt to deprive others of theirs, or impede their efforts to obtain it." *The Basic Writings of John Stuart Mill: On Liberty, The Sub-jection of Women* (New York: Random House, 2002), 14–5.

4   Stuart Ewen, *Captains of Consciousness: Advertising and the Social Roots of the Consumer Culture* (New York: Basic Books, 2001), 25.

5   John Dewey, *Democracy and Education* (Mineola, NY: Dover, 2004), 4–5.

6   Noam Chomsky, *Secrets, Lies, and Democracy*, int. David Barsamian (Tucson, AZ: Odonian Press, 1994), 36.

7   Ibid., 9.

8   Edward Bernays, *Propaganda* (New York: H. Liveright, 1928), 62.

9   Ibid., 94.

10   Fyodor Dostoyevsky, *Crime and Punishment* (Mumbai: Wilco, 2005), 24.

11   Richard Wilkinson and Kate Pickett, *The Spirit Level: Why Equality Is Better for Everyone* (New York: Bloomsbury, 2011), 75, 256. Wilkinson and Pickett's research on equality is of significance for the egalitarian outlook I promote in the last chapter of this book. In *The Spirit Level* the two epidemiologists posit that "problems in rich countries are not caused by the society not being rich enough (or even by being too rich) but by the scale of material differences between people within each society being too big. What matters is where we stand in relation to others" (25). They go on to show that the level of income inequality closely correlates with, among other things, levels of adult illiteracy, homicide rates, rates of imprisonment, teenage pregnancy, drug abuse, obesity, mental illness, and suicide rates. For indicator after indicator, Wilkinson and Pickett demonstrate the superior performance of equal societies relative to unequal ones. They note, for example, that in Canada mental illness affects 1 in 5 people while in more equal countries like Japan and Germany, less than 1 in 10 people are affected by it (67).

12   Alfred D. Chandler Jr. and Bruce Mazlish, *Leviathans: Multinational Corporations and the New Global History* (New York: Cambridge University Press, 2005), 2.

13   Ibid., 26, 135.

14   Bianca Mugyenyi and Yves Engler, *Stop Signs: Cars and Capitalism on the Road to Economic, Social and Ecological Decay* (Vancouver: RED/Fernwood Publishing, 2011), 16.

15   Ibid., 62.

16   Ibid.

17   Ibid., 186.

18   Ibid., 162.

19   Adam Smith, *The Theory of Moral Sentiments* (Minneapolis: Filiquarian Publishing, 2009), 9.

20   Peter Singer, *The Life You Can Save* (New York: Random House, 2009), 25.

21   George Orwell, *The Collected Essays, Journalism and Letters of George Orwell: My Country Right or Left*, 1940–1943, eds. Sonia Orwell and Ian Angus (London: Secker & Warburg, 1968), 258.

22   The text of, and various information related to, the leaked "Downing Street Memo" can be found online at downing-streetmemo.com.

23   "Public Attitudes Toward the War in Iraq: 2003-2008," *Pew Research Center RSS*, March 19, 2008.

24   "Newsweek Poll: What America Knows," *Newsweek*, June 23, 2007. Archived from the original by Wikipedia on August 30, 2007.

25   In the months following the invasion, Bush would declare that "the liberation of Iraq ... removed an ally of al-Qaeda." For this and other examples of such distortion by Bush administration officials, as well as refutations, see the March 2004 Congress report by the Committee on Government Reform titled "Iraq on the Record."

26   National Commission on Terrorist Attacks Upon the United States, *9/11 Commission Report* (New York: Cosimo, 2010), 62, 66.

27   Ben H. Bagdikian, *The New Media Monopoly* (Boston: Beacon Press, 2004), 3.

28   Ibid., 25.

29   Edward S. Herman and Noam Chomsky, *Manufacturing Consent: The Political Economy of the Mass Media* (New York: Pantheon, 2002).

30   Bagdikian, *The New Media Monopoly*, 23.

31   Mugyenyi and Engler, *Stop Signs*, 182–3.

32   Herman and Chomsky, *Manufacturing Consent*, 30.

33   George W. Bush, "Address to a Joint Session of Congress and the American People," US Capitol, Washington D.C., September 20, 2011, Address.

34   Quoted in Herman and Chomsky, *Manufacturing Consent*, xx.

35   Herman and Chomsky, *Manufacturing Consent*, xx.

36   Ibid., xxi. Along with giving differing treatment to the victims of friendly and enemy states when reporting on them, the media overwhelming choose to report on "worthy victims," while ignoring those who are "unworthy." Herman and Chomsky note, for instance, that in the U.S. media

> a 1984 victim of the Polish Communists, the priest Jerzy Popieluszko, not only received far more coverage than Archbishop Oscar Romero, murdered in the U.S. client-state El Salvador in 1980; he was given more coverage than the aggregate of one hundred religious victims killed in U.S. client states, although eight of those victims were U.S. citizens. (xx)

37   Despite the media's recent unwillingness to describe waterboarding as such, there should be no doubt that the technique is a form of torture. (It is also, therefore, a crime under international law.) The victim is put under severe physical stress by being denied the ability to breathe. It causes acute panic and distress, and if carried on for sustained periods of time, it can result in death. "Open Letter to Attorney General Alberto Gonzales," Human Rights Watch, April 5, 2006, www.hrw.org/news/2006/04/05/open-letter-attorney-general-alberto-gonzales.

38   Neal Desai, Andre Pineda, Majken Runquist, and Mark Fusunyan, "Torture at Times: Waterboarding in the Media,"

Joan Shorenstein Center on the Press, Politics, and Public Policy, Harvard Student Paper, April 2010.

39   Herman and Chomsky, *Manufacturing Consent*, lx.

40   Noam Chomsky, *The Common Good*, int. David Barsamian (Tucson, AZ: Odonian, 1998), 43.

41   Tina Susman, "Civilian deaths may top 1 million, poll data indicate," *Los Angeles Times*, September 14, 2007; Arwa Damon, "Iraq refugees chased from home, struggle to cope," *CNN*, June 21, 2007.

42   Bagdikian, *The New Media Monopoly*, 49.

43   From the Deepa Bhatia documentary film *Nero's Guests*.

44   Dean Nelson, "India has one third of world's poorest, says World Bank," *Telegraph*, April 18, 2013.

45   Herman and Chomsky, *Manufacturing Consent*, 17.

46   Brian Morton, "Falser Words Were Never Spoken," *New York Times,* August 30, 2011.

47   M.K. Gandhi, *An Autobiography: The Story of My Experiments With Truth* (Boston: Beacon, 1993), 58.

48   Edward Bellamy, *Looking Backward* (Coln St Aldwyn: Echo Libray, 2005), 44.

49   Catherine Aielie, "Global Advertising Spending Rose in 2010, Nielsen Says," *Bloomberg*, April 4, 2011.

50   John Kenneth Galbraith, *The Essential Galbraith* (Boston: Houghton Mifflin, 2001), 35.

51   In Upton Sinclair's 1906 novel *The Jungle*, the character Jurgis who, after leading a heartbreakingly calamitous life and eventually settling in among a group of socialists, finds that he has "a score of Socialist arguments chasing through his brain" as he goes about his day. It is not likely that many people today are, whether with socialist arguments or otherwise, "wrestling inwardly with an imaginary recalcitrant" during their daily routines. *The Jungle* (New York: Grosset & Dunlap, 1906), 386.

52 Technology, Entertainment, Design (TED) Conferences bring together academics, thinkers, philanthropists, etc. from around the world who deliver short lectures on their particular areas of expertise. The lectures are then made available to watch for free online at ted.com. As the satirical blog "Stuff White People Like" (which pokes fun at the habits of white liberals) notes, "white people will like" TED because it is "something that … allow[s] them to feel smart but doesn't require a large amount of work, time, or effort." See the post titled "#134 The Ted Conference" on stuffwhitepeoplelike.com.

53 The activist and academic Norman Finkelstein laments in a recent interview, "Ten years ago when I used to lecture, people came up to me at the end, they'd say, 'Professor Finkelstein, I read all your books.' Then, starting around four or five years ago people would line up afterwards and say, 'Professor Finkelstein, I watched all your YouTubes [sic].' And now it's reached the point where they don't even have the patience to watch a YouTube [sic] that's more than two and half minutes." I came across the interview, as it happens, on YouTube itself. See the video titled "Norman Finkelstein: 'Zionism for most people is a hairspray, a cologne'" on youtube.com.

54 David Harvey, *A Brief History of Neoliberalism* (Oxford: Oxford University Press, 2005), 198.

CHAPTER 2: INEQUALITY AND ACTIVISM

1   Martin Luther King, Jr., *A Call to Conscience: The Landmark Speeches of Dr. Martin Luther King, Jr.*, eds. Clayborne Carson and Kris Shepard (New York: Warner Books, 2001), 158.

2   Chinua Achebe, *Anthills of the Savannah* (London: Billing & Sons, 1987), 155.

3   Jason Hickel, "The truth about extreme global inequality," *Al Jazeera*, April 14, 2013.

4   Peter Singer, *The Life You Can Save* (New York: Random House, 2009).

5   Ibid., 15.

6   Ibid., 107.

7   Quoted in Narayan et al., *Voices of the Poor* (New York: Oxford UP for the World Bank, 2000), 141.

8   Denis Goulet and Michael Hudson, *The Myth of Aid*, (New York: IDOC North America, 1971), 15.

9   Hillary Rodham Clinton, "Testimony before the Senate Appropriations Committee," April 30, 2009, Available online at http://www.state.gov/secretary/rm/2009a/04/122463.htm.

10   Although the War in Afghanistan is popularly regarded as just and legal, especially when compared to its sister war in Iraq, it is illegal. The UN Security Council did not sanction it, which must be done if an aggressive war or intervention is to be deemed legal. It cannot be regarded as a defensive war either. To be considered as such the need for self-defense must be "instant, overwhelming, leaving no choice of means, and no moment of deliberation." It certainly cannot be said that there was "no moment of deliberation," as the United States waited until almost a month after the attacks of September 11, 2001, to launch the invasion of Afghanistan. See Ryan T. Williams, "Dangerous Precedent: America's Illegal War in Afghanistan," *University of Pennsylvania Journal of International Law*, 33 (2011): 563–613.

11   As Nikolas Barry-Shaw and Dru Oja Jay note, "[T]he NGO boom was fuelled by the desire of ... donors to contain the political backlash against structural adjustment and smooth the transition to neoliberalism. In the process, government officials and political and corporate elites discovered in NGOs a versatile tool." *Paved with Good Intentions: Canada's Development NGOs from Idealism to Imperialism* (Halifax: Fernwood, 2012), 31.

12   Tina Wallace, "NGO Dilemmas: Trojan Horses for Global Neoliberalism?" *The New Imperial Challenge: Socialist Register* 40 (2003), 207–8.

13   See, for instance, the numerous articles and reports on miningwatch.ca.

14   Penelope Simons and Audrey Macklin, "Defeat of responsible mining bill is missed opportunity," *Globe and Mail*, November 2, 2010.

15   Barry-Shaw and Jay also make this point in *Paved with Good Intentions*, 72.

16   Singer, *The Life You Can Save*, 35.

17   Ibid., 81–85.

18   Paul Collier, *The Bottom Billion* (Oxford: Oxford University Press, 2007), 157.

19   In *Historical Capitalism* (London: Verso, 2011), Immanuel Wallerstein explains the creation, and continuing reinforcement, of the global division of labor as follows:

> The concentration of capital in core zones created both the fiscal base and the political motivation to create relatively strong state-machineries, among whose many capacities was that of ensuring that the state machineries of peripheral zones became or remained relatively weaker. They could thereby pressure these state-structures to accept, even promote, greater specialization in their jurisdiction in tasks lower down the hierarchy of commodity chains, utilizing lower-paid work-forces and creating (reinforcing) the relevant household structures to permit such work-forces to survive. Thus did historical capitalism actually create the so-called historical levels of wages which have become so dramatically divergent in different zones of the world-system. (32)

20   Chinua Achebe, *Things Fall Apart* (New York: McDowell, Obolensky, 1959), 58–59.

21   Karl Polanyi, *The Great Transformation: The Political and Economic Origins of Our Times* (New York: Farrar & Rinehart, 1944), 164.

22   Mike Davis, *Late Victorian Holocausts: El Nino Famines and the Making of the Third World* (London: Verso, 2002).

23   "Not a solution, but aid for Somalia can save lives," *Vancouver Sun*, July 21, 2011.

24   The full name of the group is Harakat al Shabab al Mujahi-
     deen, meaning "Movement of the Striving Youth."

25   Paul Peachey, "UN lying over Somalia famine, say Isla-
     mists," *Independent*, 23 July 2011, Web.

26   Africa Watch Committee, *Somalia: A Government at War with
     Its Own People*, (New York: Africa Watch Committee, 1990),
     9. Africa Watch is a part of Human Rights Watch. In the text I
     cite the latter as the author of the report because readers will
     be more familiar with HRW than with Africa Watch.

27   Ibid., 11.

28   Quoted in Tariq Ali, *Clash of Fundamentalisms: Crusades, Ji-
     hads and Modernity* (London: Verso, 2002), 305.

29   Alex de Waal, "U.S. War Crimes in Somalia," *New Left Re-
     view* I/280 (July–August 1998): 143. At one point UN troops
     attacked a hospital in the capital, Mogadishu, on the purport-
     ed basis that a high value target had taken up refuge inside
     it. The hospital was battered by artillery shells and rockets,
     and then stormed by troops. An unknown number of patients
     and hospital staff died during the assault. A few Somali snip-
     ers had stationed themselves on the roof of the building, but
     this could hardly serve as a justification for the crushing force
     employed by UN troops—not to mention the lack of warning
     and protection given to the civilians inside the hospital. The
     man being sought, incidentally, was not found. When ques-
     tioned about the legality of the attack on the hospital, a U.S.
     military attorney reportedly told de Waal that since the UN
     was not a signatory to the Geneva Conventions it was not sub-
     ject to them (138–40).

30   Ibid., 132.

31   American troops withdrew completely a year earlier, in March
     1994. The October 3, 1993, Battle of Mogadishu, dramatized in
     the film *Black Hawk Down*, took the wind out of the U.S. war
     machine. Eighteen American soldiers were killed that day, and
     one was taken prisoner. The sense of defeat was heightened by
     the news coverage that followed, aligning U.S. public opin-
     ion against the intervention. The undertaking in Somalia, and
     the October 3 battle in particular, is remembered in American

intellectual and public discourse as a tragedy for the soldiers who fought and died during it. As de Waal points out, there is little sympathy for the innocent Somalis who lost their lives. During the Battle of Mogadishu, for instance, 200 or more Somalis, many of them civilians, were killed as a result of the massive amounts of firepower employed by U.S. troops. The total number of innocent dead during the entire intervention will likely never be known. Assessing the American strategy in Somalia, de Waal asks the following question: "does the U.S. Army no longer fight but rather massacre?" (ibid., 144).

32   Quoted in Michael Maren, *The Road to Hell* (New York: Free Press, 1997), 287.

33   Much of what follows about Somalia is derived from Jeremy Scahill, *Dirty Wars: The World Is a Battlefield* (New York: Nation Books, 2013).

34   This was being done, incidentally, in breach of an arms embargo the U.S. itself had originally helped to impose on Somalia (ibid., 260).

35   Scahill notes that it is not clear when al-Shabab was formed. It could have been in as early as the late 1990s, or as late as 2006. He cites one source that points to 2003 as the most likely date of formation (ibid., 236).

36   Ibid., 264.

37   Ibid., 271.

38   Canada gave a substantial amount of aid to Ethiopia before and after the invasion, failing to make the aid contingent upon the withdrawal of Ethiopian troops from Somalia. Yves Engler, *The Black Book of Canadian Foreign Policy* (Vancouver: Red Publishers, 2009), 200.

39   Scahill, *Dirty Wars*, 278.

40   Ibid.

41   "American Public Vastly Overestimates Amount of U.S. Foreign Aid," *WorldPublicOpinion.org*, November 29, 2010.

42 Thom Hartmann, *Unequal Protection: How Corporations Be-came "People" and How You Can Fight Back* (San Francisco: Berrett-Koehler, 2010), 144.

43 Léonce Ndikuma and James K. Boyce, *Africa's Odious Debts* (London: Zed, 2011), 64.

44 Ibid., 53–54.

45 Ibid., 55.

46 Singer, *The Life You Can Save*, 32–33.

47 Ibid., 99.

48 Narayan et al., *Voices of the Poor*, 49.

49 Abhijit Banarjee and Ester Duflo, *Poor Economics* (New York: Public Affairs, 2011), 80.

50 As Abhijit Banarjee and Esther Duflo report, when they began surveying the poor about their aspirations for their children they found that "the most common dream of the poor is that their children become government workers ... The poor don't see becoming an entrepreneur as something to aspire to. The emphasis on government jobs, in particular, suggests a desire for stability, as these jobs tend to be very secure even when they are not very exciting" (ibid., 226–27).

51 Quoted in Ha-Joon Chang, *23 Things They Don't Tell You About Capitalism* (New York: Bloombury Press, 2010), 162.

52 Phil Cain, "Microfinance meltdown in Bosnia," *Al Jazeera,* January 4, 2010. Lydia Polgreen and Vikas Bajaj, "India Mi-crocredit Faces Collapse from Defaults," *New York Times,* November 17, 2010.

53 See chapter 15 in Chang, *23 Things They Don't Tell You About Capitalism.*

54 Quoted in Noam Chomsky, *Year 501* (London: Verso, 1993), 104.

55 Mike Davis, *Planet of Slums* (New York: Verso, 2006), 144–46.

56 Oscar Wilde, *The Soul of Man Under Socialism* (London: A. L. Humphreys, 1912), 3.

57 Quoted in Raj Patel, *Stuffed and Starved* (Brooklyn: Melville House, 2008), 83.

58 Amartya Sen, *Development as Freedom* (Oxford: Oxford University Press, 1999), 23.

59 Richard Wright, *Black Boy (American Hunger)* (New York: Harper Perennial, 2008), 312.

CHAPTER 3: CLIMATE CHANGE AND ACTIVISM

1 David Harvey, *A Companion to Marx's Capital* (London: Verso, 2010), 21.

2 Jared Diamond, *Guns, Germs and Steel* (New York: W. W. Norton & Company, 1999), 42–44.

3 Jan Zalasiewicz et al., "Are We Now Living in the Anthropocene?" *GSA Today* 18 (2008): 5.

4 Ibid.

5 World Wide Fund for Nature, *Living Planet Report 2012 Biodiversity, Biocapacity and Better Choices,* (Gland, Switzerland: World Wide Fund for Nature, 2012), 18.

6 James Hansen, *Storms of My Grandchildren: The Truth about the Coming Climate Catastrophe and Our Last Chance to Save Humanity* (New York: Bloomsbury, 2009), 47–48.

7 In case anyone is worried about it, there is no chance that such natural "climate forcings" could bring about an ice age from this point on in human history. As Hansen notes, "Forces instigating ice ages ... are so small and slow that a single chlorofluorocarbon factory would be more than sufficient to overcome any natural tendency toward an ice age" (ibid., 37).

8 David Spratt and Philip Sutton, *Climate 'code red': The case for a sustainability emergency* (Fitzroy: Friends of the Earth, 2008), 11.

9 Quoted in Kofi Annan et al., *The Anatomy of a Silent Crisis* (Geneva: Global Humanitarian Forum, 2009), 10.

10 Fiona Harvey, "Climate Change Is Already Damaging Global Economy, Report Finds," *Guardian*, September 26, 2012; Annan et al., *The Anatomy of a Silent Crisis*, 9–11.

11 Spratt and Sutton, *Climate 'Code Red'*, 5.

12 NASA's James Hansen once advocated that warming be kept below 1.7 °C, but has more recently rescinded even this target, calling it "a disaster scenario." *Storms of My Grandchildren*, 142.

13 Alister Doyle, "World Needs to Axe Greenhouse Gases by 80 pct: Report," Reuters, April 19, 2007.

14 Hansen, *Storms of My Grandchildren*, 254.

15 John Abraham, "New Study Links Global Warming to Hurricane Sandy and Other Extreme Weather Events," *Guardian*, June 22, 2015.

16 "United Nations Framework Convention on Climate Change," United Nations, 1992, Available online at http://unfccc.int/resource/docs/convkp/conveng.pdf.

17 George Monbiot, "Selling Indulgences," *Guardian*, October 19, 2006, Available online at monbiot.com.

18 Monbiot discusses other problems with tree planting, including the fact that it is practically impossible to determine how much carbon dioxide a tree will sequester over its life. "Buying Compacency," *Guardian*, January 17, 2006, Available online at monbiot.com.

19 Doug Struck, "Buying carbon offsets may ease eco-guilt but not global warming," *Christian Science Monitor*, April 20, 2010.

20 Elisabeth Rosenthal and Andrew W. Lehren, "Profits on Carbon Credits Drive Output of a Harmful Gas," *New York Times*, August 8, 2012.

21 Patrick Bond, *Politics of Climate Justice: Paralysis Above, Movement Below* (Scottsville: University of Kwazulu-Natal, 2012).

22 Quoted in ibid., 20. Appraising the outcome in Copenhagen, Bond notes that "on behalf of mainly white capitalists, the world's rulers stuck the poor and future generations with vast clean-up charges—and worse: certain death for millions" (26).

23 Quoted in ibid., 114.

24 Ibid., 27.

25 Ibid., 35.

26 See "Global Greenhouse Gas Emissions Data," epa.gov.

27 See the webpage titled "Ten Sources of Greenhouse Gas," knowledge.allianz.com

28 Bianca Mugyenyi and Yves Engler, *Stop Signs: Cars and Capitalism on the Road to Economic, Social and Ecological Decay* (Vancouver, B.C.: Red/Fernwood), 116, note ii.

29 Hugh McKenna, "Global Auto Sales up 6 per cent So Far in 2012: Scotiabank," *Globe and Mail*, August 14, 2012.

30 Mugyenyi and Engler, *Stop Signs*, 114.

31 World Wide Fund for Nature, *Living Planet Report*, 38.

32 "Livestock a Major Threat to Environment," *FAONewsroom*, November 29, 2006.

33 See the webpage titled "EPA Green Buildings," epa.gov.

34 Hansen, *Storms of My Grandchildren*, 174–75.

35 "Livestock a major threat to environment" *FAONewsroom*, November 29, 2006.

36 Vernon Ruttan, "Is War Necessary for Economic Growth?" *Historically Speaking* 7 (July/August 2006), 17–19. Ruttan explains, for instance, the development of the Boeing 707:

    > Boeing engineers began to consider the possibility of developing a commercial jet airliner in the late 1940s. It was considered doubtful that initial sales could justify development costs. The problem of financing development costs for what became the Boeing 707 was resolved when Boeing won an Air Force contract to build a military jet tanker designed for in-flight refueling of the B-52 bomber (17).

37 John H. Richardson, "Keystone," *Esquire*, August 12, 2012. See "Athabasca Oil Sands Project – Scotford Upgrader and Quest CCS," shell.ca.

38 Quoted in Fred Magdoff and John Bellamy Foster, *What Every Environmentalist Needs to Know about Capitalism* (New York: Monthly Review Press, 2011), 121.

39 David Harvey, *The Enigma of Capital: And the Crises of Capitalism* (London: Profile Books, 2011), 40.

40 Ibid., 26–27.

41 Richardson, "Keystone."

42 Dan Eggen and Kimberly Kindy, "Three of Every Four Oil and Gas Lobbyists Worked for Federal Government," *Washington Post*, July 22, 2010. Also cited in Mugyenyi and Engler, *Stop Signs*, 195.

43 The MMS has since been disbanded, its responsibilities being taken over by the Bureau of Ocean Energy Management and the Bureau of Safety and Environmental Enforcement.

44 "The Oil Industry Spent $72.5 Million Lobbying Congress in 2006 Alone." Mugyenyi and Engler, *Stop Signs*, 195.

45 Joe Romm, "Obama's Worst Speech Ever: 'We've Added Enough New Oil And Gas Pipeline to Encircle the Earth'," March 22, 2012.

46 Seth Hanlon, "Big Oil's Misbegotten Tax Gusher," *Center for American Progress*, May 5, 2011.

47 "Big Oil's Bogus Campaign," *New York Times*, March 30, 2012.

48 See "New API Ad Campaign Stresses Energy Tax Hikes Could Increase Pain at the Pump," api.org.

49 Hanlon, "Big Oil's Bogus Campaign."

50 Quoted in Maxwell Boykoff and Jules Boykoff, "Balance as Bias: Global Warming and the US Prestige Press," *Global Environmental Change* 14 (2004), 124.

51 Ibid., 129.

52 Ibid., 131.

53 Ibid., 131–32.

54 Ibid., 134.

55   Frank Newport, "Americans' Global Warming Concerns
     Continue to Drop," *Gallup Politics*, March 11, 2010.

56   If funding for REDD is based on international carbon mar-
     kets, the scheme will suffer from the fact that "offsetting," as
     noted earlier in the chapter, does nothing to reduce overall
     global emissions.

57   John Vidal, "UN's forest protection scheme at risk from or-
     ganised crime, experts warn," *Guardian*, October 5, 2009.

58   Chris Lang, "WWF scandal (part 3): Embezzlement and
     evictions in Tanzania," Web log post, *red-monitor.org*, May
     9, 2012.

59   Betsy A. Beymer-Farris and Thomas J. Bassett, "The REDD
     Menace: Resurgent Protectionism in Tanzania's Mangrove
     Forests," *Global Environmental Change* 22 (2012), 333. Also cit-
     ed in Chris Lang, "WWF scandal (part 3)."

60   Beymer-Farris and Bassett, "The REDD Menace," 334.

61   Karl Polanyi, *The Great Transformation: The Political and Eco-
     nomic Origins of Our Times* (New York: Farrar & Rinehart,
     1944), 178.

62   Ibid., 73.

CHAPTER 4: THE WAY FORWARD

1   Karl Marx, Capital: A *Critique of Political Economy*, Volume
     I, trans. Ben Fowkes (London: Penguin Classics, 1990), 171.

2   My retelling of Zahhak's story is based on Helen Zimmern's
     1883 translation of the epic: Firdawsī, *The Epic of Kings: Sto-
     ries Retold from Firdusi*, trans. Helen Zimmern (London: T.F.
     Unwin, 1883). However, the name spellings I use are the
     ones I have encountered on Wikipedia—I suspect that these
     are more commonly used today.

3   Firdawsī, *The Epic of Kings*, 7.

4   Ibid., 10.

5   Bertrand Russell, *Political Ideals* (New York: The Century Co., 1917), 7–8.

6   Ibid., 9.

7   Ibid.

8   Ibid., 14–5.

9   Possessive desires have come to proliferate so widely that their associated evils end up encroaching on the territory of creative desires:

> If one man has found a cure for cancer and another has found a cure for consumption [i.e. tuberculosis], one of them may be delighted if the other man's discovery turns out a mistake, instead of regretting the suffering of patients which would otherwise have been avoided. In such cases, instead of desiring knowledge for its own sake, or for the sake of its usefulness, a man is desiring it as a means to reputation (ibid., 10).

10   M. K. Gandhi, *Hind Swaraj*, ed. Anthony Parel (New York: Cambridge University Press, 1997), 31–32.

11   M.K. Gandhi, *India of My Dreams* (Delhi: Rajpal & Sons, 1959), 26.

12   See, for instance, the discussion in the third chapter of David Graeber's *The Democracy Project: A History, a Crisis, a Movement* (New York: Spiegel & Grau, 2013). For James Madison's view of democracy, see papers 10, 14, and 48 in *The Federalist Papers*.

13   James Madison, "The Federalist No. 14," *The Federalist Papers*, ed. Roy P. Fairfield (Baltimore: John Hopkins University Press, 1981), 24.

14   Tom Shine, "47% of Congress Members Millionaires—a Status Shared by Only 1% of Americans," ABC News, November 16, 2011.

15   Gregory Korte and Fredreka Schouten, "57 Members of Congress among Wealthy 1%," *USA Today*, November 16, 2011.

16   Arthur Cottrell, ed., *The Penguin Encyclopedia of Classical Civilization* (London: Viking, 1993), 89.

17   Graeber, *The Democracy Project*, 115.

18   Ibid., 114.

19   From the Anand Patwardhan documentary film *Jai Bhim Comrade*. I have made one slight alteration to the English translation of the song as it appears in the subtitles of the film. I have decided to use "*Raises prices*, encourages black money" instead of "*Increases inflation*, encourages black money."

20   Graeber, *The Democracy Project*, 159.

21   Many of those who stand in elections in the Third World openly rely on paternalism to achieve success. This is certainly the case in my native Pakistan. Even in rich countries, though it may be covered with a sophisticated veneer, the practice is not altogether absent.

22   Graeber, *The Democracy Project*, 159.

23   Ibid., 184–85.

24   George Orwell, *A Collection of Essays* (Orlando, FL: Houghton Mifflin Harcourt, 1970), 314.

25   Noam Chomsky, *What Uncle Sam Really Wants* (Berkeley, CA: Odonian Press, 1992), 92.

26   As Chomsky puts it, the point of such propaganda was "to undermine the popular belief that there really might be progress towards a more just society with democratic control over its basic institutions and concern for human needs and rights." Ibid.

27   George Orwell, *Homage to Catalonia* (Orlando, FL: Houghton Mifflin Harcourt, 1952), 104.

28   Michael Lebowitz, *The Socialist Alternative: Real Human Development* (New York: Monthly Review Press, 2010), 66.

29   Ibid., 52–54.

30   Lebowitz makes this point somewhat more eloquently with the help of Karl Marx. Quoting Marx, he relates that we are forced to make use of the "estranged language of material values" in order to hold onto dignity (ibid., 67).

31   Karl Polanyi, *The Great Transformation: The Political and Economic Origins of Our Times* (New York: Farrar & Rinehart, 1944), 46.

32   Ibid., 71.

33   Ibid.

34   Ibid., 75.

35   Albert Einstein, *Out of My Later Years* (Westport, CT: Greenwood Press, 1970), 124.

36   Martin Luther King, Jr., *A Call to Conscience: The Landmark Speeches of Dr. Martin Luther King, Jr.* eds. Clayborne Carson and Kris Shepard (New York: Warner Books, 2001), 157–58.

37   Ibid., 141.

38   King remarked in a speech delivered in New York on April 15, 1967 that "there are twice as many Negro soldiers dying in action in Vietnam as whites in proportion to their numbers in the population." The speech is available online at www.crmvet.org/docs/mlkviet2.htm. Black soldiers accounted for almost 1 in 5 deaths in Vietnam from 1961 to 1966 even though they made up less than 10 percent of military. After facing large amounts of criticism over this point, the U.S. military made substantive efforts to lower the proportion of deaths among black soldiers and by the end of the war in 1975 the proportion of black soldiers killed in the war amounted to 12 percent of total deaths. See the article "African Americans in the Vietnam War" by David Coffey. Originally from the *Encyclopedia of the Vietnam War*, the article can be accessed online at www.english.illinois.edu/maps/poets/s_z/stevens/africanamer.htm.

39   King, *A Call to Conscience*, 143.

40   Ibid., 142.

41   Ibid., 158.

42   Ibid., 157.

43   Quoted in Vincent Harding, *Martin Luther King, the Inconvenient Hero* (Maryknoll, NY: Orbis Books, 2008), 19.

44   Quoted in Mark Engler, "Dr. Martin Luther King's Economics: Through Jobs, Freedom," *Nation*, February 1, 2010.

45   Quoted in Harding, *Martin Luther King*, 162.

46   Peter Kropotkin, *The Conquest of Bread* (Cambridge: Cambridge University Press, 1995), 74.

AFTERWORD

1   bell hooks, *Feminism Is for Everybody* (Cambridge, MA: South End Press, 2000), viii.

2   Ibid., 16.

3   Ibid., 32.

4   Ibid., 36.

5   Peter Custers, *Capital Accumulation and Women's Labour in Asian Economies* (New York: Zed Books, 1997), 145.

6   Ibid., 154.

7   hooks, *Feminism Is for Everybody*, 46.

8   "Line 9 Oil Pipeline Opening Said to Be Delayed until a New Federal Government Is in Place," *Burlington Gazette*, August 18, 2015.

9   Howard Zinn, *You Can't Be Neutral on a Moving Train* (Boston: Beacon Press, 2002), 146.

10   There are, of course, important differences between Gandhian civil disobedience and the kind we most often practice today. Gandhi's approach involved breaking unjust laws and *welcoming the fury of the state*, including baton charges, arrests, detainment, and criminal sentencing. Most of us who take up civil disobedience today, including myself, do not seem to have the resolve to welcome the repression that comes with breaking laws and custom. We would rather avoid facing rubber bullets, arrest, and criminal proceedings.

11   Perry Anderson, *The Indian Ideology* (New York: Verso, 2013).

12   There were a fair number of things about Gandhi himself
      that should be subjected to criticism: his dressing up of
      politics in a religious garb; his misogyny; his misappropri-
      ation of radical rhetoric; the irresponsible position he took
      in response to the demands made by the Dalit community;
      and his willingness to set aside nonviolence when it suited
      him (as in the case of Kashmir) are noteworthy examples.
      But, despite the sometimes troubling nature of his deci-
      sions and his overall approach, no one would deny that his
      invaluable contributions to the independence struggle offer
      important lessons for activists today.

13   Quoted in Peter Linebaugh, *Stop, Thief!* (Oakland, CA: PM
      Press, 2014), 132.

ABOUT THE AUTHOR

Umair Muhammad is a researcher who focuses
on the political economy of climate change. He
organizes with Jane-Finch Actions Against Poverty
in Toronto and his writing has appeared in *Climate
& Capitalism*, *Briarpatch* magazine and others.